LINCOLN
AND
HIS CONTEMPORARIES

Abraham Lincoln
(Courtesy of *The Abraham Lincoln Museum*)

LINCOLN
AND
HIS CONTEMPORARIES

Edited by
Charles M. Hubbard

MERCER UNIVERSITY PRESS

1979   1999

TWENTY YEARS OF PUBLISHING EXCELLENCE

ISBN 0-86554-627-4
MUP/H470

© 1999 Mercer University Press
6316 Peake Road
Macon, Georgia 31210-3960

10 9 8 7 6 5 4 3 2 1

∞The paper used in this publication meets the minimum requirements
of American National Standard for Information Sciences.

Library of Congress Cataloging-in-Publication Data

Lincoln and his contemporaries / edited by Charles M. Hubbard.
p. cm.
Includes bibliographical references (p.) and index.
ISBN 0-86554-627-4
1. Lincoln, Abraham, 1809-1865—References with generals—
Congresses. 2. Lincoln, Abraham, 1809-1865—Relations with
Afro-Americans—Congresses. 3. Lincoln, Abraham, 1809-1865—
Adversaries—Congresses. 4. Lincoln, Abraham, 1809-1865—
Portraits—Congresses. 5. United States—Politics and
government—1861-1865—Congresses. I. Hubbard, Charles M.,
1939- .
E457.2.A142   1999
973.7'092—dc21   98-50768
                                  CIP

TABLE OF CONTENTS

Introduction   1
    by Charles M. Hubbard

1. Abraham Lincoln: Commander-in-Chief or Attorney-in-
     Chief   11
    by Frank Williams

2. "That Attractive Rainbow": The Image of Abraham
     Lincoln as Commander-in-Chief   39
    by Harold Holzer

3. Lincoln and Halleck   69
    by John Y. Simon

4. Lincoln and Race Relations   87
    by Hans L. Trefousse

5. "Something More Than the Mere 'Union' to Fight For":
     African-Americans Respond to
     Lincoln's Wartime Policies   101
    by Edna Greene Medford

6. Why Booth Shot Lincoln   121
    by Terry Alford

7. Shooting the President as a Military Necessity   139
    by William Hanchett

8. The Creation of an American Myth:
     The Assassination of Abraham Lincoln   149
    by Thomas R. Turner

This book is dedicated to

Henry S. Spencer, M. D.,

in appreciation of his years of generous and committed friendship to the Abraham Lincoln Museum.

ACKNOWLEDGMENTS

All the participants in this project thank Lincoln Memorial University and the Abraham Lincoln Museum for sponsoring the symposium that produced these essays. The museum staff, particularly Frank Coburn, Terina Collins, and Charles Vial, worked diligently to ensure the success of this extraordinary event. We are especially indebted to LaVerne Neal for her patient and conscientious proofing and preparation of the manuscript. Finally, a special thanks to Marc A. Jolley and the staff at Mercer University Press for their enthusiastic commitment to the success of this volume.

CONTRIBUTORS

Charles M. Hubbard, Ph.D., is Associate Professor of History at Lincoln Memorial University in Harrogate, Tennessee, where he also serves as the Executive Director of the Abraham Lincoln Museum. His books include *The Burden of Confederate Diplomacy* and *The Many Faces of Lincoln*.

Terry Alford, Ph.D., is Professor of History at Northern Virginia Community College. He is the author of *Prince Among Slaves*, and is the Editor of *John Wilkes Booth: A Sister's Memoir*.

Judge Frank J. Williams is an Associate Justice of the Superior Court of Rhode Island and is a leading authority on Abraham Lincoln. He served nine years (1976-1985) as President of the Abraham Lincoln Association. His publications include *Abraham Lincoln: Sources and Style of Leadership*.

Harold Holzer is Chief Communications Officer of the Metropolitan Museum of Art and is a leading authority on the political culture of the Civil War era. He has written and edited over ten books including *The Lincoln-Douglas Debates*, and has written over 250 articles for popular magazines and scholarly journals.

Thomas R. Turner, Ph.D., is Professor of History at Bridgewater State College and is Editor-in-Chief of the Lincoln Herald. He is the author of *Beware the People Weeping: Public Opinion and the Assassination of Abraham Lincoln*. He is a recognized authority on the assassination conspiracies of Lincoln.

William Hanchett, Ph.D., is Professor of History at San Diego State University. His books include *Out of the Wilderness: The Life of Abraham Lincoln* and *The Lincoln Murder Conspiracies*.

Edna Greene Medford, Ph.D., is Associate Professor of History at Howard University and Associate Director for History of the African Burial Ground Project. Her articles have appeared in *Slavery and Abolition*, the *Virginia Magazine of History and Biography*, and other scholarly journals.

John Y. Simon, Ph.D., is Executive Director of the Ulysses S. Grant Association and has edited twenty-two volumes on *The Papers of Ulysses S. Grant*. He is Professor of History at Southern Illinois University.

Hans Trefousse, Ph.D., is a distinguished Professor Emeritus of History of Brooklyn College and the Graduate Center of the City University of New York. He is author of biographies of Thaddeus Stevens, Andrew Johnson, and others, notably, *Lincoln's Decision for Emancipation*.

INTRODUCTION

ABRAHAM LINCOLN AND
HIS CONTEMPORARIES

The essays in this book are about Abraham Lincoln and the response of three identifiable, yet very different, groups of his contemporaries to the president's wartime policies. The essayists explore the motivation for and the implications of many of Lincoln's strategies and policies. The reaction by individuals, often leaders, within each of these identifiable groups reveals the ideological foundations that are a part of the post-Civil War American experience. An examination of the interaction of Abraham Lincoln with his contemporaries also contributes to our understanding of this extraordinarily complex man.

The book is organized into three sections that generally follow in chronological order and reflect the level of activity at various periods. Although the constituencies under consideration are continually involved throughout the war, the influence of each is more pronounced at different times. For example, the interaction between Lincoln and his generals is examined first, followed by the African American experience, and finally, Lincoln's assassination.

The material included here, along with the idea to publish it, developed from the Centennial Lincoln Symposium at Lincoln Memorial University in April of 1997. The contributions of the Civil War president and his contemporaries to modern society hold great interest for a wide range of people. It is fitting that the legacy of Abraham Lincoln be acknowledged and studied in an environment created to provide a "living memorial to Abraham Lincoln," as General Oliver Otis Howard stated the mission of the University when he founded it in 1897. The sub-theme of the conference, "Lincoln and His Contemporaries," allowed scholars to present the results of a broad range of recent scholarship and revisit the conclusions of previous historians and writers spanning Lincoln's presidency and the Civil War years.

As Americans search for relevance and meaning in the Civil War experience, it is impossible to separate the issues relating to Lincoln from the war. Issues relating to equality, the role of government, and democracy remain open-ended questions. Much as today's Americans, Lincoln and his contemporaries struggled with these monumental questions, and their answers and actions redefined the United States. In a recent speech, Arthur M. Schlesinger, Jr. declared that American democracy must be flexible in order to survive in the modern world.[1] Undoubtedly, today's America would surprise Lincoln, but the basic values associated with his legacy are fundamental to American thought and the value system that has affected United States policy, both at home and abroad.

The Civil War began almost immediately after Lincoln's inauguration, and one of his first challenges was to locate and appoint competent generals to lead the Federal army in subduing the rebellion. This was Lincoln's first serious encounter with the military, having only very limited experience during the Black Hawk War.[2] The new president was extraordinarily sensitive to both the political and military requirements of those he selected for command positions, but it was well into the war before he was able to identify generals that would fight and lead competently in the field. Lincoln was sensitive to his dual role as leader of the civil government and commander-in-chief of the armed forces. All of these problems complicated the task of locating competent commanders, and some of his most difficult decisions involved his attempts to secure a competent General of the Army.[3]

---

[1] Arthur M. Schlesinger, Jr., speech "American Democracy Past and Present" delivered to the Institute of American Studies, University of London, November 1997.

[2] David Herbert Donald, *Lincoln* (New York: Simon & Schuster, 1995).

[3] T. Harry Williams, *Lincoln and His Generals* (New York: Knopf, 1952).

different order in book

I
Holzer

In the first of three essays devoted to the relationship of Lincoln to his generals, Harold Holzer analyzes the changing military image in the public mind of Lincoln as the war progressed. With the use of contemporary printed images, Holzer traces and identifies three distinctly different public images of Lincoln. First, he suggests that during the first two years of his administration, Lincoln was perceived as a weak and possibly even a cowardly president. However, after a military victory at Antietam and the decision to issue the Emancipation Proclamation, there was a distinct shift toward respectability in the depiction of Lincoln in lithographs, prints, and caricatures. Finally, after his assassination, contemporary artists tend to deify and define the president as much more than an ordinary hero. The changing relationship of Lincoln to his generals and the direct relationship of victory or defeat in the images depicted by commercial artists are clear. Moreover, Holzer identifies the relationship of popular opinion on art and the effect of art on public opinion.

Lincoln dealt with the failure and success of his generals, their dismissal, appointment, and overall direction with sensitivity and compassion. Judge Frank Williams, in "Abraham Lincoln: Commander-in-Chief or Attorney-in-Chief," demonstrates that many of these skills were developed during Lincoln's career as a practicing attorney. Williams is eminently qualified to analyze these aspects of Lincoln's relationship to his generals, not only because of his lifelong study of Lincoln, but also because of his many years as a practicing attorney and Superior Court Judge. Even though Lincoln had little military experience, he quickly grasped the broad military strategy and recognized early that the Rebel armies must be defeated before the Union could be reconstructed. The failure of Union generals to gain early success in the East caused the president great distress and disappointment. Williams argues that, despite his sadness over the human tragedy caused by mounting casualty reports, the president remained patient and sympathetic with those in command, even while searching for more effective commanders. Lincoln, as a successful practicing attorney on the Illinois frontier circuit, refined his extraordinary common sense

Williams

and intuitiveness into a remarkable ability to deal with people from all social and economic levels of society. The need to compromise and negotiate settlements for his clients contributed enormously to the president's ability to gain the support and ultimately the goodwill of his generals and political contemporaries. Williams concludes that these skills enabled the president to lead a nation in war and redefine the American political and military system.[4]

Simon

Further illustrating Lincoln's remarkable ability to deal effectively with a wide range of personalities, John Y. Simon inves-tigates the role of General Henry Halleck within the command structure of Lincoln's war effort. In an intriguing essay, Simon suggests that the otherwise incompetent Halleck acted as a buf-fer, deflecting and accepting criticism of the overall military strategy that might otherwise have been directed toward the commander-in-chief. The president would have been less popular, and therefore less effective, had he not allowed General Halleck such an inauspicious role. Simon strongly disagrees with the conclusions of Stephen Ambrose in his sympathetic biography of Halleck, and states that the "otherwise incompetent general served Lincoln very well in this capacity."[5] Lincoln often called on Halleck for military advice, once he returned to Washington from Tennessee, but the general usually refrained from recommendations. In his publicly defined role as chief military adviser to the president, Halleck must be considered as ineffective.[6] Simon demonstrates that Lincoln tended to capitalize on Halleck's otherwise disastrous career to broaden his political base that contributed substantially to his ability to govern and maintain public support for the war effort.

As much as any identifiable group of Lincoln's contemporaries, African Americans were dramatically affected by

---

[4] Charles M. Hubbard, "The Chicken Bone Case," in *American History Magazine*, October (1997): 31-69. This case illustrates Abraham Lincoln's understanding of his contemporaries and how best to communicate with them. Donald (*Lincoln*, 51) points out the patient and personal nature of Lincoln the lawyer.
[5] Stephen E. Ambrose, *Halleck: Lincoln's Chief of Staff* (Baton Rouge: Louisiana State University Press, 1962).
[6] T. Harry Williams, *Lincoln and His Generals*.

Lincoln's wartime policies. In the first of two essays focusing on the African American experience and Abraham Lincoln's relationship with them, Hans L. Trefousse states that Lincoln believed in and reflected liberal attitudes and ideas toward race relations. Trefousse, professor of history at Brooklyn College of the City University of New York, reinforces his previously stated position in his biography of Andrew Johnson, that Lincoln's assassination contributed substantially to the failure of radical reconstruction. He argues persuasively that the racism reflected in the policies of Andrew Johnson contradicted Lincoln's ideas toward the rights of African Americans in a reformed Union. He denounces Johnson and his reconstruction policy because it was motivated by racism and white supremacy. Comparing the speeches and writings of Lincoln and Johnson, Trefousse concludes that Lincoln's liberalism, at least by nineteenth century standards, is easily identifiable, and that Lincoln's reconstruction policies would have prevented the divisions and frustrations within the post-Civil War government.

Edna Greene Medford, in the second essay on the African American experience, acknowledges that the Emancipation Proclamation was a step toward fulfilling the dreams and expectations of African Americans by freeing some of the slaves, and identifies the failure of Lincoln to address the demands of all blacks for equality under the law. Medford, professor of history at Howard University, is an authority on the African American experience during the Civil War and Reconstruction. She identifies in the essay the disappointments and frustrations felt by a significant group of Lincoln's contemporaries. The failure of liberal Republicans to address problems of equality beyond freedom from slavery created lasting unrest for African Americans. She suggests that the inability of white American politicians to accept the concept of equality accounts for the failure of reconstruction to permanently protect black civil rights in general and suffrage in particular. Both these essays identify the Emancipation Proclamation as only one step in the pursuit of equal rights and protection under the Constitution. However, it allowed 250,000 freed blacks to enlist and fight in the Union army and to secure freedom from slavery for

themselves and future generations. The most significant contribution of the Emancipation Proclamation, according to Medford,
was the opportunity for African Americans to participate in the
complete emancipation effort. She maintains that the racism of
Lincoln and his victorious contemporaries remained entrenched
and helped sustain laws and attitudes that were discriminatory
and hateful toward African Americans and other minorities.

The war, emancipation, Lincoln's assassination, and subsequent radical reconstruction dramatically affected Southern
whites as well as African Americans. The old planter aris-
tocracy, if it was to survive in the reconstructed Union in any
form, needed to accommodate the new economic structure that
emerged after the war. The necessity to make these day-to-day
accommodations reached across all class lines in the South. At
least as important, as Willie Lee Rose pointed out, was the need
to jettison the long established belief in "benevolent pater-
nalism, the Biblical patriarch at the center of a stable and
orderly agrarian world." For these people, the old world was
gone and the relationships that the antebellum South took for
granted had to be rethought. When referring to the Southern
oligarchy, Rose states that "nothing less than [their] own
significance in the only world [they] knew was at stake."[7] The
world that African Americans had known was also gone. It was
clear enough that they were no longer slaves, but what freedom
actually meant was a larger matter. Freedom meant the absence
of slavery with all its violence and coercion, restraints and
humiliations. However, it was necessary for African Americans
to preserve and expand the definition of freedom. Moreover,
African Americans could not allow the features of slavery to be
reimposed under any new guise. Despite the use of their
newfound freedoms to defend their rights, eventually the white
Southern leadership would impose limitations on the new
freedom. As Leon Litwack has pointed out, despite these
humiliating restrictions, slavery no longer existed as defined by
the "absence of any freedom."[8] The destruction of slavery was

---

[7] Willie Lee Rose, "Masters without Slaves" in William W.
Freehling, ed., *Slavery and Freedom* (New York: Oxford University
Press, 1982) 76.
[8] Leon Litwack, *Been in the Storm Too Long* (New York: Knopf, 1979).

legally accomplished by the Thirteenth Amendment, but the positive contributions of Abraham Lincoln to the process cannot be denied. The quest for equality for all Americans, particularly those introduced to the United States through the institution of slavery, continues.

The war and emancipation changed forever the social structure within the Southern states that were forcibly reconstructed into the Union. No matter how violently they resisted, they ultimately failed in their attempts to create a slaveholder's republic. From the ranks of the pro-slavery sympathizers, there emerged a group committed to terrorism and assassination. The conspiracy plots and assassination of Abraham Lincoln are the subject of the final three essays.

Professor Terry Alford, of Northern Virginia Community College, profiles Lincoln's assassin, John Wilkes Booth. He carefully reviews the life of the successful American actor and sees Booth as a committed reactionary seeking to create political and military disruption that he hoped would allow the pro-slavery elements to retain control of the Confederate government and maintain an army in the field. Alford points out that, unlike Jefferson Davis and other Southern leaders, Booth was a fanatic who felt Lincoln's murder would avenge the lost Southern cause if it failed to accomplish his larger objective to continue the Southern rebellion. He demonstrates that while Booth was a fanatic, he was no fatalist, and believed that the possibility existed for continued resistance to the Union attempts to destroy his way of life.

William Hanchett, professor emeritus at San Diego State University, argues that Booth was part of a larger conspiracy that reached to the highest levels of the Confederate government in Richmond. He explains that various conspiracy plots to assassinate the president were part of the broader context of Confederate resistance and accelerated both in number and in intensity as battlefield losses mounted and the Southern cause became more desperate. He argues that his analysis of Confederate and Union documents discovered after the war proves the Confederate government explored a number of abduction plots. He further contends that John Wilkes Booth received direct financial and other assistance from the official Confederate government. Professor Hanchett analyzed the larger conspiracy theory in *The Lincoln Murder Conspiracies* first published in 1983. A recent study by William A. Tidwell entitled *April '65* supports Hanchett's conclusions by arguing that the Confederate secret service used gold reserves to fund various capture plots. By analyzing official documents, corre-spondence, and financial records, a strong case can be made for Confederate involvement with John Wilkes Booth and his assassination team.[9]

Not surprisingly, many historians believe that John Wilkes Booth acted alone or at least within a small personalized group of operatives he recruited. In the final essay in this section, Thomas Turner, editor of the *Lincoln Herald* and professor of history at Bridgewater State College, suggests that there is no direct evidence to support a larger conspiracy theory. Turner claims that no hard evidence exists directly linking Booth to any organized Confederate sponsored conspiracy, and believes only circumstantial evidence can be used to support the larger conspiracy claim of Hanchett and Tidwell. In a broader sense, this essay relates Lincoln's assassination to subsequent presidential assassinations and murder plots. Over the years, historians and writers have presented numerous theories about the assassination of Lincoln; therefore, historians will continue to debate and seek answers to the many intriguing and mysterious questions associated with the assassination of President Lincoln.

Many commentators have called the American Civil War the ultimate breakdown in democracy. The inability of Americans to accept government by a majority over a substantial minority represents the failure of the democratic process.[10] Lincoln recognized the need to prevent the demolition of democratic government. The determination of Lincoln and the American people to preserve and protect, through the use of force, the democratic

---

[9] William Hanchett, *The Lincoln Murder Conspiracies* (Urbana and Chicago: University of Illinois Press, 1983; William A. Tidwell, *April '65: Confederate Covert Action in the American Civil War* (Kent, OH: The Kent State University Press, 1995).
[10] William E. Gienapp, *The Origins of the Republican Party, 1852-1856* (New York: 1987); see also Gienapp, "Political System and the Coming of the War" in Gabor S. Boritt, ed., *Why the Civil War Came* (New York: Oxford University Press, 1996).

experiment contributes substantially to the role of the United States as the protector of democracy, freedom, and equal opportunity in today's world. Although Lincoln was no abolitionist and tended to dislike the radicalism of the movement, he was certainly a progressive liberal when viewed from a mid-nineteenth century perspective. His views on the ability of the people to govern themselves and his commitment to free labor combined with his belief in capitalism to shape not only the future of the United States, but through future generations of Americans, the modern world.

1

ABRAHAM LINCOLN: COMMANDER-IN-CHIEF OR ATTORNEY-IN-CHIEF

By Frank Williams

Because more is known about Abraham Lincoln's legal practice than ever before, historians risk the temptation of focusing too much on his legal career and not enough on the fact that for Lincoln, the law was in many respects only a means to politics, his first love. It is necessary to remember that the sixteenth president is unique among the forty-one men who have served in the Oval Office: he ran for political office at a younger age and earlier in his career than any other lawyer-president. And, Lincoln was one of the few who ran for office *before* he became a lawyer. Although he was defeated in his first effort to become a state legislator, the effort signaled that Lincoln's greatest satisfaction in life ultimately would come from working on political problems facing his community. It is ironic that the youthful Lincoln first attempted to emulate George Washington, his first political hero, by running for office following military experience. In the end, he spent too little time on his initial political campaign because, like Washington, he was attempting to gain military experience while competing for public office. He never repeated that mistake. Lincoln would take a different road to political success.

According to Thomas A. Bailey's study of presidential greatness, "The American people admire a chieftain who can command their allegiance, inspire them to greater patriotism, and arouse them with a challenge that will appeal to their

Figure 1. Calender print of *Lincoln The Candidate,* painted by Reynolds Jones for the Chicago & Illinois Midland Railway. Politics beckoned a youthful Lincoln. He ran for political office at a younger age than any other lawyer-president. (Courtesy of The Frank & Virginia Collection of Lincolniana.)

Figure 2. Calender print of *Lincoln-The Circuit Rider* painted by Reynolds Jones for the Chicago & Illinois Midland Railway. For Lincoln, politics and law were mutual careers. (Courtesy of The Frank & Virginia Collection of Lincolniana.)

better selves."[1] All of this, Abraham Lincoln did successfully, using skills he honed in the courtroom. The purpose of this paper is to suggest how Lincoln never wavered from his primary life goal of exercising political leadership. The essay will also show also how Lincoln used the law as his springboard to reach his larger political goals and how this contributed to his later success as president and commander-in-chief.

Abraham Lincoln was able to blend the traditional differences between the law and politics into a singular democratic vision. By temperament he was not a radical like Chief Justice Roger B. Taney, the judicial activist who undid Congressional compromises. Nor was he a typical lazy lawyer-president like James Buchanan. Lincoln was a full-fledged politician who was willing to find solutions to public policy issues — including the divisive issues of civil war and slavery — when Taney and others would provoke them due to their ideological extremism, narrow legal approach, and lack of political experience.

Lincoln the Warrior

Apart from showing that Lincoln did indeed adopt George Washington as a role model, Lincoln's military experience in a way encouraged him to pursue a legal career, based on his contact during military service with the individual who later became his law partner and a state legislator. Election as a captain in the state militia by his men provided Lincoln the first public acceptance that he would seek continually in political life. Though the Black Hawk Indian War provided Lincoln a minimally challenging military experience especially compared to Washington's, it linked him with a successful military campaign, even if his personal contribution to it came mostly, he admitted, in fighting mosquitoes.[2] Importantly, Lincoln's

---

[1] Thomas A. Bailey, *Presidential Greatness* (New York: Irvington Publishers, 1978) 223.
[2] *The Collected Works of Abraham Lincoln*, Roy P. Basler, ed. (New Brunswick: Rutgers University Press, 1953) 1:510 (hereinafter *Collected Works*).

military service encouraged him to study the law as a means to further his political ambition.

Lincoln the Lawyer

A basic fact that must be kept at the forefront in considering Lincoln's career is that Lincoln did not practice law and *then* become a politician. Not only was he a politician first, he was always both a politician and a lawyer simultaneously. This differentiates him from many politicians and lawyers. There can be little question that Lincoln's long, arduous, and intensive practice of the law at the Bar of Illinois, along with his political career, constituted his principal schooling and preparation for later presidential duties, including the role of commander-in-chief, which were thrust upon him. It proved dynamic training.

His twenty-four-year legal-political career before he assumed the presidency suggests six lessons. First, his legal career demonstrates unending energy–especially when considering that Lincoln expended equal, concurrent energy in politics. Second, his legal-political career demonstrated that Lincoln had the ability to juggle effectively more than one job at the same time. Third, the study of law and his work in the legislature allowed him to develop and hone his political skills. Fourth, the law allowed him to develop his oral and written skills. Fifth, the law also gave him time to reflect and to learn about human nature and the broader purpose of democratic life. Ultimately, Lincoln's dual careers provided him the kind of broad background that assured him the potential for growth as a politician, which was always his ultimate goal. It would insure that he not only would be a commander-in-chief or an attorney-in-chief, but that he would evolve as America's finest political leader. Sixth, Lincoln had a great sense of timing, knowing when to undertake an issue and when to be Machiavellian.

Unending Energy: A Dual Career

Lincoln's legal career demonstrated his unending energy, especially when one understands that he remained politically

Figure 3. Print of *Lincoln the Circuit Rider* from an oil painting by Bonhajo. Original in the Abraham Lincoln Museum, Lincoln Memorial University, Harrogate, Tennessee. Lincoln rode the circuit as an attorney, amassing career appearances in more than 5,000 cases and 333 plus appeals before the Illinois Supreme Court (Courtesy of The Frank & Virginia Collection of Lincolniana.)

Figure 4. Calender print of *Lincoln The Lawyer*, painted by Fletcher C. Ransom for the Chicago & Illinois Midland Railway. Lincoln's law practice ranged from complex corporate problems to determing the owner of a pig. (Courtesy of The Frank & Virginia Collection of Lincolniana.)

active. Like many successful lawyers, Lincoln boasts an abundance of physical and mental energy. He was more than an ordinary lawyer when he practiced on the 8th Judicial Circuit. After all, how many attorneys, either in Lincoln's day or today, can claim a career spanning twenty-four years, handling more than five thousand cases, and appearing in over 333 cases before the supreme court of his state?[3] All this and politics too.

The Juggler: Multiple Roles

His legal-political career demonstrated that Lincoln had the ability to juggle more than one job at the same time. Any practicing attorney must be able to handle more than one case at a time. They must deal with different cases, strategies and ideas. Lincoln proved himself to be a masterful juggler, handling a heavy legal practice and a demanding schedule as a working legislator and emerging leader of his party. Performing multiple tasks at the same time later would prove essential in the presidency, which requires an individual to manage multiple roles: commander-in-chief, chief executive, chief diplomat, party leader, legislative leader, and leader of the American people.

Analytical Skills: Wheat from Chaff

The study of law and his work in the legislature allowed Lincoln to develop and hone his political skills. The study of law demands skill in separating principles from facts. Lincoln did not get lost among the trees. His years of legal practice taught him to beware of stumps and to search for underlying principles. Indeed, he came to appreciate the fact that the law, politics and life have deeper meanings. Lincoln was a complex spirit.

---

[3] Statistics from the Lincoln Legal Papers Project, Illinois State Historical Library, Springfield, Illinois.

Communication Skills: The Vision Issue

The law allowed Lincoln to hone his oral and writing skills. Lincoln's dual legal and political careers provided him with a unique opportunity to improve his inclination to search for the best way to communicate meaning. He never ceased working to improve his writing, including his ability to construct verse. As a result of his fascination with words, he developed a poetic understanding of the law, politics, and life. He had a philosophical disposition.

Lifelong Learner: An Autodidact

The law also gave him time to think and to learn about both human nature and the broader purpose of democratic life. Lincoln was not a specialist (few existed in his day) but he was a well-rounded lawyer with a comprehensive practice encompassing a variety of legal problems. These included cases as diverse as the validity of a slave as consideration for a promissory note, enforcement of gambling debts, seduction, guardianship, foreclosure of mortgages and mechanics liens, divorce, specific performance, county seat wars, ejectment, wills, the defense and sometimes the prosecution of cases, personal injuries, libel and slander, injunction, replevin, patents, taxation, insurance, partition, statute of frauds, eminent domain, trusts and trustees, constitutional law, real estate and procedure at law and equity. At times, he even served as acting circuit judge.[4]

His political-legal training afforded him great insight into human nature and allowed him time to ruminate about the larger issues facing his times. He learned to frame legal cases into a broader setting.

The lessons that Lincoln learned from his dual political-legal career can be illustrated through several episodes. His prior training and background assured that Lincoln would take a broad view of most issues and try to flesh out the facts in his effort to achieve his ultimate political goal.

---

[4] John J. Duff, *Abraham Lincoln Prarie Lawyer* (New York: Rinehart & Company, 1960).

(6) Sense of Timing

Both as a lawyer and part-time lawyer-judge, Lincoln developed a judicious, sometimes even Machiavellian, sense of timing. He learned that legal matters are sometimes best when left alone. In a sense he probably would have been a judicial restrainist if he had served full-time on the bench. Wise justices know when not to become involved in a political quagmire.

As a lawyer who fully understood the bigger political context in which the law operates, Lincoln learned when to lead and when to let public opinion ripen. He was the master Machiavellian in the best sense of that term, understanding that leaders operate within a small window of opportunity. His legal-political background honed his skills. He knew when to seize the initiative and when to let matters ripen. Inexperienced lawyers and those without political experience fail to appreciate this crucial dimension of successful leadership

Lincoln's dual career would ultimately provide him with the broad kind of background that would assure him the potential to grow as a politician. It would ensure that he would not only be a commander-in-chief or an attorney-in-chief; he would grow into America's finest political leader.

The Issue of Slavery: A Constitutional or a Moral Question

In contrast to Roger B. Taney's training in the law, Lincoln's experience taught him that there were multiple levels of meaning and that a literal approach would diminish the broader political meaning of a document. For example, in an 1857 speech he fully admitted the economic, constitutional, and biblical dimensions of the slave question, and yet summed up the situation with a broader moral:

> In those days, by common consent, the spread of the black man's bondage to new countries was prohibited; but now, Congress decides that it *will* not continue the prohibition, and the Supreme Court decides that it *could* not if it would. In those days, our Declaration of Independence was held sacred by all, and thought to

include all; but now, to aid in making the bondage of
the Negro universal and eternal, it is assailed, and
sneered at, and construed, and hawked at, and torn,
till, if its framers could rise from their graves, they
could not at all recognize it. All the powers of the earth
seem rapidly combining against him. Mammon is after
him; ambition follows, and philosophy follows, and the
Theology of the day is fast joining the cry. They have
him in his prison house; they have searched his person,
and left no prying instrument with him. One after
another they have closed the heavy iron doors upon
him, and now they have him, as it were, bolted in with
a lock of a hundred keys, which can never be unlocked
without the concurrence of every key; the keys in the
hands of a hundred different men, and they scattered to
a hundred different and distant places; and they stand
musing as to what invention, in all the dominions of
mind and matter, can be produced to make the
impossibility of his escape more complete than it is.[5]

And then his answer to all the defenses of slavery: economic,
philosophic, humanitarian, and religious: he summarized as
follows:

The ant who has toiled and dragged the crumb to his
nest will fiercely defend the fruit of his labor against
whatever robber assails him. So plain, that the most
dumb and stupid slave that ever toiled for a master
does constantly know that he has been wronged. So
plain that no-one, high or low, ever does mistake it,
except in a plainly selfish way; for, although, volume
upon volume is written to prove slavery is a very good
thing, we never hear of the man who wishes to take the
good of it, by being a slave himself.[6]

[5] Basler ed., *Collected Works*, 2:404.
[6] Ibid., 222.

Lincoln could reason to broader principles rather than limit himself to previous precedents. His political values always allowed him to consider another interpretation. Life for Lincoln was a many-layered thing. His legal experience reinforced that view.

The Appointment of Hooker: Balancing

Lincoln's ability to weigh both sides was illustrated by the way he handled the ambivalent appointment of Major General Joseph Hooker to command the Army of the Potomac in 1863. The previous commander, Major General Ambrose E. Burnside had brought an order dismissing four of his general officers, including General Hooker, charging him with "unjust and unnecessary criticisms of the actions of his superior officers..."[7] But the order required presidential approval. Lincoln's alternative was to accept Burnside's resignation. Having long realized that Burnside's dismissal was inevitable, Lincoln had decided in favor of Hooker, but the selection did not come without misgivings. The day after Hooker's appointment, Lincoln confessed to Senator Orville H. Browning that he was not satisfied with Hooker's conduct, but knew of no better choice.[8] Lincoln's most explicit avowal of his reservations, however, came from his own pen in this lawyer-like letter to Hooker, replete with contrasting points of view:

Executive Mansion
Washington, January 26, 1863

Major General Hooker:
General.
I have placed you at the head of the Army of the Potomac. Of course I have done this upon what appear to me to be sufficient reasons. And yet I think it best for

---

[7] William Marvel, *Burnside* (Chapel Hill: University of North Carolina Press, 1991) 215.
[8] Basler ed., *Collected Works*, 6:79.

you to know that there are some things in regard to which, I am not quite satisfied with you. I believe you to be a brave and a skillful soldier, which, of course, I like. I also believe you do not mix politics with your profession, in which you are right. You have confidence in yourself, which is a valuable, if not an indispensable quality. You are ambitious, which, within reasonable bounds, does good rather than harm. But I think that during General Burnside's command of the Army, you have taken counsel of your ambition, and thwarted him as much as you could, in which you did a great wrong to the country, and to a most meritorious and honorable brother officer. I have heard, in such a way as to believe it, of your recently saying that both the Army and the Government needed a Dictator. Of course it was not for this, but in spite of it, that I have given you the command. Only those generals who gain successes, can set up dictators. What I now ask of you is military success, and I will risk the dictatorship. The government will support you to the utmost of its ability, which is neither more nor less than it has done and will do for all commanders. I much fear that the spirit which you have aided to infuse into the Army, of criticizing their Commander, and withholding confidence from him, will now turn upon you. I shall assist you as far as I can, to put it down. Neither you, nor Napoleon, if he were alive again, could get any good out of an army, while such a spirit prevails in it.

And now, beware of rashness–Beware of rashness, but with energy, and sleepless vigilance, go forward, and give us victories.

Yours very truly

A. Lincoln[9]

One cannot help but note how Lincoln gave all the positive reasons for the appointment, followed by his concerns, and ending with both support and admonition. Lincoln's political-

[9] Ibid., 6:78-79.

legal experience had taught him to take reasonable risks and to deal best with what he had at the moment. This letter to Hooker also demonstrates excellent personnel management skills that are indispensable to leadership. The subsequent disastrous Battle of Chancellorsville notwithstanding, the letter had the desired result. "That is just such a letter as a father might write to his son. It is a beautiful letter...," said Hooker to a friend when he received Lincoln's letter. "After I have got to Richmond, I shall give that letter to you to have published."[10] To that end he went to work energetically, reorganizing the Army of the Potomac. Depleted ranks were filled, strenuous drill instituted, and damaged morale restored. By April 1863, the troops were ready for the offensive.

The Case of Meade: Retaining Composure

When General George G. Meade telegraphed the news of Lee's crossing the Potomac to Henry W. Halleck on 14 July 1863, the general-in-chief replied that "the escape of Lee's army without another battle has created great dissatisfaction in the mind of the president, and it will require an energetic pursuit on your part to remove the impression that it has not been sufficiently active heretofore."[11] Stung, Meade telegraphed Washington and asked to be relieved of command. In a letter intended to mollify him, President Lincoln wrote Meade on 14 July: "I have just seen your despatch to General Halleck, asking to be relieved of your command, because of supposed censure of mine. I am very–very–grateful to you for the magnificent success you gave the cause of the country at Gettysburg; and I am sorry now to be the author of the slightest pain to you..."[12]

---

[10] Noah Brooks and Herbert Mitgang, eds., *Washington in Lincoln's Time* (New York: Rinehart & Company, 1958) 57-58.
[11] *The War of the Rebellion: A Compilation of the Official Records of the Union and Confederate Armies* (Washington, DC: US Government Printing Office, 1880-1901), xxvii, pt. 3:687; pt. 1:667.
[12] Basler ed., *Collected Works*, 6:327-328.

But Lincoln could not hide his disappointment and the tone shifted.

> Again my dear general, I do not believe you appreciate the magnitude of the misfortune involved in Lee's escape. He was within your easy grasp, and to have closed upon him would, in connection with our late successes, have ended the war. As it is the war will be prolonged indefinitely. If you could not safely attack Lee last Monday, how can you possibly do so South of the river, when you take with you very few more than two thirds of the force you had in hand? It would be unreasonable to expect, and I do not expect you can now effect much. Your golden opportunity is gone, and I am distressed immeasurably because of it....[13]

Lincoln began his letter with praise before relating his criticism. In another lawyer-like maneuver, the angered president put the letter aside and never sent it, discerning its probable effect on Meade and the Army. One is reminded of Captain Harry Truman who as commander-in-chief would blow off steam by writing letters he never sent.

Appointment of Political Generals: Alexander Schimmelfennig

In his approach to the issue of political generals, Lincoln's tack was as direct as it might have been in an argument before the Illinois Supreme Court. The president well understood the difference between national strategy and military strategy. National strategy shapes a nation's political goals in wartime while military strategy uses armed forces to achieve these political goals. Most studies of Lincoln and his generals focus on the military strategy. But it is impossible to understand military strategy without comprehending political war aims for which military strategy is merely the instrument. It is especially true

[13] Ibid.

in the Civil War which was preeminently a political war precipitated by a presidential election in a highly politicized society,
fought largely by volunteer soldiers who elected many of their
officers and who also helped elect the political leadership who
ran the war effort and from whom many of the commanders
were appointed for political reasons.

Many military historians have criticized the political
generals, citing the case of one appointment in particular. To
satisfy a large German constituency in the North, Lincoln
appointed a number of German-American generals. Looking at
a list one day in 1862, Lincoln saw the name of Alexander
Schimmelfennig. When Secretary of War Edwin M. Stanton
protested that better candidates were available, the president
was insistent upon Schimmelfennig. "His name," said Lincoln,
"will make up for any difference there may be,"[14] and he
walked away repeating the name Schimmelfennig with amuse-
ment. Schimmelfennig turned out to be a mediocre general. But
those who criticize his appointment solely on military grounds
miss the broader point recognized clearly by Lincoln the
perceptive "political" lawyer. The president made the appointment for reasons of national strategy. Each political general
represented an important ethnic, regional, or political constituency whose support was critical to the war effort. To mobilize
German-American support, Lincoln had to give them political
patronage.

Emancipation as a Military Measure

Another illustration of Lincoln's concentric legal and political
grasp of issues came with emancipation. The problem was
prodigious. Nothing in the Constitution authorized the
Congress or the president to confiscate property without
compensation. When the preliminary Emancipation Proclamation was issued on 22 September 1862, declaring slaves in

---

[14] T. Harry Williams, *Lincoln and His Generals* (New York: Alfred A.
Knopf, 1952) 11.

Figure 5. *Union* engraved by H. S. Sadd, published by William Pate, New York. 1852. Lincoln was a successful commander-in-chief thanks to his constituitional "bending" within the framework of his wise temperament. (Courtesy of The Frank & Virginia Collection of Lincolniana.)

Figure 6. Chromolithograph *President Lincoln Writing the Proclamation of Freedom*, January 1st, 1863. [Peter E.] Ehrgott, [Adolphus] Forbriger & Co., after a painting by David Gilmore Blythe and published by M. Dupuy, Pittsburg, 1864. Lincoln became the resident lawyer of his administration dealing with emancipation, West Virginia statehood, conscription, suspension of the privilege of the writ of habeas corpus, and many other constitutional questions. (Courtesy of The Frank & Virginia Collection of Lincolniana.)

the states still in rebellion to be free the next 1 January, the legal basis of the action seemed obscure. Lincoln cited two acts of Congress for justification. Occupying a large part of the proclamation, they had little to do with the subject, indicating that Lincoln had not really settled in his own mind the issue of his power to act. But when the time came for the final Emancipation Proclamation on New Year's Day 1863, Lincoln had determined that his act was a war measure taken as commander-in-chief to weaken the enemy.

"Now, therefore, I, Abraham Lincoln, president of the United States by virtue of the power in me vested as commander-in-chief of the Army and Navy of the United States, in time of actual armed rebellion against the authority and government of the United States, and as a fit and necessary war measure for suppressing said rebellion, do...order and declare that all persons held as slaves within said designated States and parts of States are, and henceforward shall be free..."[15]

The proclamation may have had all "the moral grandeur of a bill of lading,"[16] as one historian complained, but the basic legal argument for the validity of his action could be understood by everyone. And his sense of timing was perfect. To James Conkling, a critic, he wrote, "You dislike the Emancipation Proclamation, and perhaps would have it retracted. You say it is unconstitutional. I think differently. I think the Constitution invests its Commander-in-Chief with the law of war. The most that can be said--if so much--is that slaves are property. Is there--has there ever been--any question that by the law of war, property, both of friends and enemies, may be taken when needed? And is it not needed whenever taking it helps us, or hurts the enemy?"[17] This exemplifies Lincoln who consistently took the shortest distance between two legal points.

[15] Basler ed., *Collected Works*, 6:29-30.
[16] Richard Hofstadter, *The American Political Tradition* (New York: Vintage Books, 1974) 169
[17] Basler ed., *Collected Works*, 6:408.

The proposition as a matter of law may be argued. But it is not the law upon which this analysis focuses, but rather Lincoln's political and legal approach to it. Lincoln saw the problem with the same logical directness with which he saw most problems: a commander-in-chief may under military necessity take property. Slaves are property. As the commander-in-chief and because there is a military necessity, the property is taken.

Lincoln's legal logic is also evident in his letter to Conkling: "You say you will not fight to free negroes. Some of them seem willing to fight for you; but, no matter. Fight you, then, exclusively to save the Union. Whenever you shall have conquered all resistance, if I shall urge you to continue fighting, it will be an apt time, then, for you to declare you will not fight to free negroes."[18]

Lincoln's military strategy matured and eventually encompassed both the Eastern and Western theaters of operation. His common sense made him a great strategist as he was clever enough to keep troops in the West who had been raised in the West and sending other troops to the Eastern theater.

Just as he moved to implement military strategy, he moved to adopt an extension and logical consequence of his Emancipation Proclamation. In 1863 he announced that those slaves freed by the proclamation would "be received into the armed service of the United States to garrison forts, positions, stations, and other places."[19] In this way Lincoln planned for manpower difficulties to be significantly eased by this new source of soldiers, "the great available and as yet unavailed of, force for the restoration of the Union."[20] Lincoln realized that arming Southern blacks, "to whatever extent the negroes should cease helping the enemy, to that extent it weakened the enemy... I thought that whatever negroes can do as soldiers, leaves just so much less for white soldiers to do, in saving the Union... But negroes, like other people, act upon motives. Why should they do any thing for us, if we will do nothing for them? If they stake their lives for us, they must be prompted by the strongest

[18] Ibid., 409.
[19] Ibid., 30.
[20] Ibid., 149.

motive–even the promise of freedom. And the promise being made, must be kept."[21] Lincoln correctly believed that the program weakened the enemy in another way: psychologically. He thought that "the bare sight of fifty thousand armed, and drilled black soldiers on the banks of the Mississippi, would end the rebellion at once."[22] He did not believe that the rebellion could survive if such a black military force could "take shape, and grow, and thrive, in the South."[23]

The Doctrine of Necessity: No Hamlet

Lincoln supported a doctrine of necessity. In his view, the civil courts were powerless to deal with individual insurrectionists. Lincoln noted, "he who dissuades one man from volunteering, or induces one soldier to desert, weakens the Union cause as much as he who kills a Union soldier in battle. Yet this dissuasion, or inducement, may be so conducted as to be no defined crime of which any civil court would take cognizance."[24] He knew that a president had to act.

In his most famous passage on the subject, he stated, as if writing a brief, "Must I shoot a simple-minded soldier boy who desserts, while I must not touch a hair of a wily agitator who induces him to desert? This is nonetheless injurious when effected by getting a father, or brother, or friend in a public meeting, and there working upon his feelings until he is persuaded to write the soldier boy that he is fighting in a bad cause, for a wicked administration of a contemptible government, too weak to arrest and punish him if he so deserts. I think that, in such a case, to silence the agitator and save the boy is not only constitutional, but withal a great mercy."[25]

Lincoln's legal arguments on the power of necessity in wartime can be found in his notes to guide General Benjamin F. Butler in the occupation of Norfolk. Lincoln's legalistic view was

---

[21] Ibid., 409.
[22] Ibid., 149-50.
[23] Ibid., 158.
[24] Ibid., 264.
[25] Ibid., 266.

that "[n]othing justifies the suspending of the civil by the military authority, but military necessity, and of the existence of that necessity the military commander, and not a popular vote, is to decide. And whatever is not within such necessity should be left undisturbed."[26]

Lincoln believed he had the legal power to do that, which in his judgment, was necessary to achieve a purpose. On the other hand, power that was unnecessary for the task at hand, he could comfortably turn down. Lincoln always operated within the constraints of the law recognizing that power in a democracy always requires checks and balances. On the other, he refused to retreat to his bed and pull the covers over his head in times of crisis.

Delegated Authority in Politics and Law

Lincoln's dual career in the world of politics and law taught him essential lessons in how to succeed in democratic politics. He learned this from his legislative and legal career. From his multiple law partners he learned to dislike inequality among professionals, so that from his first to final partnership he insisted on establishing a firm based on friendship. He treated Billy Herndon the way he was not treated in his own first firm as a new lawyer. One suspects that Herndon's admiration for Lincoln grew proportionately to this treatment, even if Lincoln's one habit of reading aloud drove him to distraction, not to speak of the mutual dislike between him and Mary Lincoln. All legal revenue was divided equally between Lincoln and Herndon even if Mary complained about her spouse's partner.

In the presidency Lincoln simply applied what he had learned as a legislator and lawyer to the presidential office. He would willingly delegate authority both in civil and military matters if his associates demonstrated competence. His greatest success in this regard was working out that personal line of demarcation between when to command and when to delegate; what to keep in his own hands and what to assign to others.

[26] Basler ed., *Collected Works*, 7:47-48.

As commander-in-chief, Lincoln was careful to distinguish clearly between when he was giving orders and when he was making recommendations, when he expected to be obeyed and when he wished his views merely to be considered. In giving a military analysis to General Don Carlos Buell he said, "I have not offered, and do not now offer them as orders; and while I am glad to have them respectfully considered, I would blame you to follow them contrary to your own clear judgment–unless I should put them in the form of orders."[27] This is almost like an attorney cajoling, rather than a commander issuing orders.

As commander-in-chief, Lincoln was not perfect. The very type of suggestions made to General Buell would sometimes land him in trouble; they were not free from ambiguity. He sometimes allowed his generals too much discretion in putting plans into action, and he did nothing when some of them casually ignored his directives. Caving in to political pressures, he often meddled at the wrong time.

Yet no one could fault his analytical thinking, developed and sharpened by Lincoln's legal practice. On 1 July 1854 he wrote, "If 'A' can prove, however conclusively, that he may, of right, enslave 'B'–why may not 'B' snatch the same argument, and prove equally, that he may enslave 'A'? You say 'A' is white, and 'B' is black. It is *color*, then; the lighter, having the right to enslave the darker? Take care. By this rule, you are to be slave to the first man you meet, with a fairer skin than your own. You do not mean *color* exactly? You mean the whites are *intellectually* the superiors of the blacks, and, therefore have the right to enslave them? Take care again. By this rule, you are to be slave to the first man you meet, with an intellect superior to your own."[28] Compare this with his letter to General Don C. Buell on 13 January 1862, written while General George B. McClellan was ill: "...I state my general idea of this war to be that we have the *greater* numbers, and the enemy has the greater facility of concentrating forces upon points of collision;

---

27 Ibid., 5:98.
28 Ibid., 2:222-23.

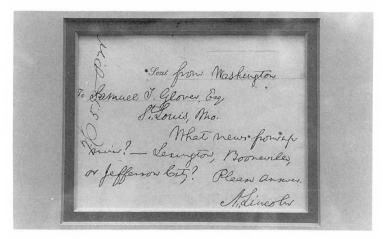

Figure 7. Telegram to Abraham Lincoln's lawyer friend, Samuel T. Glover, September 28, 1861, *Collected Works of Abraham Lincoln*, vol. 4, p. 538. Lincoln's legal training insured succinct messages, like this telegram, while President. His query "What news?" was an ongoing effort during the Civil War to determine the facts. (Courtesy of The Frank & Virginia Collection of Lincolniana.)

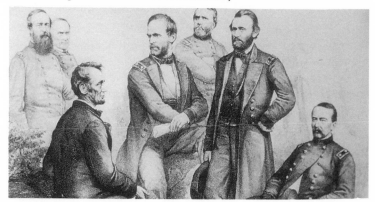

Figure 8. Lithograph *Lincoln and His Generals* printed by A[lphonse], Brett and published by Jones & Clark, New York, and C. A. Asp, Boston, 1865. As commander-in-chief. Lincoln finally found generals who would fight and follow his leadership and policy for winning the war. With Ulysses S. Grant, Lincoln found a kindred spirit who understood that he as general-in-chief must not infringe on the authority of the commander-in-chief. (Couresy of The Frank & Virginia Collection of Lincolniana.)

that we must fail, unless we can find some way of making our advantage an over-match for his; and that this can only be done by menacing him with superior forces at different points, at the same time; so that we can safely attack, one, or both, if he makes no change; and if he weakens one to strengthen the other, forbear to attack the strengthened one, but seize. and hold the weakened one gaining so much..."29 Both letters are excellent examples of Lincoln's formal analytical way of thinking.

Finally, he found Ulysses S. Grant, a general who needed neither suggestions nor orders. Yet Grant understood that he must not, however great the powers invested in him as commander, infringe on the authority of the president. When one of his first meetings as commanding general produced deadlock with Secretary of War Stanton, Stanton warned that he would have to take Grant to the president. Grant agreed and acknowledged that the president outranked both of them.30 President and general had already established the proprieties of their relationship. "All [I] had wanted," Lincoln told him at their first private interview, "and had ever wanted was someone who would take responsibility and act, and call on [me] for all the assistance needed, pledging [myself] to use all the powers of government in rendering such assistance."31 Nonetheless, the president did not depend on a formal system of delegation to subordinates, even those whom he trusted. On the great matters of public policy, Lincoln left no doubt that the president was in charge of the Lincoln administration. In September 1861, John C. Fremont, commander of Union forces in the border state of Missouri, proclaimed martial law in the state and declared the slaves of all Confederate sympathizers free. General David Hunter did the same the following spring in the Department of the South–the states of South Carolina, Georgia, and Florida where there were a few Union

---

29 Ibid., 5:98.
30 Bruce Catton, *Grant Takes Command* (Boston: Little, Brown and Company, 1969) 139.
31 Don E. Fehrenbacher and Virginia Fehrenbacher, eds., *Recollected Words of Abraham Lincoln* (Stanford: Stanford University Press, 1996) 179.

beachheads along the coast. Lincoln revoked both military edicts because he feared alienating the Southern Unionists he was still cultivating, especially those in the border states of Kentucky, Missouri and Maryland. Lincoln considered these states crucial to maintenance of the Union. He would like to have God on his side, he reportedly said, but he must have Kentucky, and Fremont's emancipation order would probably "ruin our rather fair prospect of Kentucky"[32] if he let the order stand.

By the end of the war General Grant had earned the president's great trust. But when at various times, Grant was in contact with the enemy, Lincoln reminded him "not to decide, discuss, or confer upon any political question. Such questions the president holds in his own hands; and will submit them to no military conferences or conventions."[33] What emerges from this pattern is another of Lincoln's fundamental legal prin-ciples–a dividing line between what could be delegated and what could not.

His legal theories of emancipation as a military measure, his treatment of his commanders and the preservation and dele-gation of authority were direct and aimed at problem solving. While the problems were, of course, different from the problems Lincoln solved as a practicing lawyer, the incisive logic used in their solution was much the same. Similarly, Lincoln drew from the practice of law his incredible industry and his indefatigability. His qualities developed from his wide experience representing all kinds of people in all kinds of cases.

His letter to General Joseph Hooker on 5 June 1863 while the Army of the Potomac was shadowing the Army of Northern Virginia heading north toward Pennsylvania is just the kind of common sense that one would expect from a good lawyer. "In one word, I would not take any risk of being entangled upon the river, like an ox jumped half over a fence, and liable to be torn by dogs, front and rear, without a fair chance to gore one way or kick the other."[34]

[32] Basler ed., *Collected Works*, 4:506.
[33] Ibid., 8:330-31.
[34] Ibid., 6:249.

Fact Finding: The Legal Mind

Lincoln absorbed information by using lawyer-like interrogatories. When he sought the advice of General Winfield Scott on the Fort Sumter crisis, he told the general, "You will much oblige me by giving answers, in writing, to the following interrogatories." He proceeded to ask three questions: "How long could the fort hold out without supplies or reinforcements? Could these things be supplied within that time, and what help would be needed to do this?"[35] These followed his law office technique to the point that he customarily finished his questions, as he did here, by asking the witness to tell him whatever else they knew about the matter. He asked the old general, "Please answer these, adding such statements, information, and counsel as your great skill and experience may suggest."[36]

When his plan of attack differed from that of General McClellan's, he directed him to answer a series of very direct questions: "Wherein is a victory more certain by your plan than mine?"[37] He underlined his key words just as he had in his legal interrogatories years before.

He used the same approach in face-to-face contacts. After the Battle of Antietam, Lincoln moved discreetly to see if McClellan was involved in any scheme to replace him as president. There had been such rumors in the army because Lincoln was to issue an Emancipation Proclamation. McClellan in turn wondered about the president's support of him as Lincoln had sent only meager congratulations after the battle. So McClellan sent Allan Pinkerton, his chief of intelligence, to the White House thinking he could ferret information out of the president. From Pinkerton, Lincoln learned a great deal more than the intelligence chief thought he was revealing. Using cross examination techniques which he had perfected at the bar,

[35] Ibid., 4:279.
[36] Ibid.
[37] Basler ed., *Collected Works*, 5:118-19.

Lincoln quizzed Pinkerton in an unobtrusive manner until he had convinced himself that Antietam had not been a great victory but a lost opportunity.[38]

Sometimes he had to render an actual legal opinion. There is no finer example of Lincoln acting as lawyer-judge than his review of the sentences of 303 Sioux who had been condemned to be hanged for their alleged role in the Minnesota uprising. Even though the verdicts were received enthusiastically throughout Minnesota, Lincoln was determined to separate the murderers and rapists from those who had simply joined in the battles. Reviewing each case, he found much of the evidence to be insufficient. The president narrowed the list to thirty-eight, writing each condemned Indian's name in his scrupulously-careful decision.[39]

Conclusion

Commenting on the power of colonial lawyers at the time of our Revolution, Edmund Burke declared in one of his great speeches: "This study [of law] renders men acute, inquisitive, dexterous, prompt in attack, ready in defense, full of resources. No other profession is more closely connected with actual life than the law. It concerns the highest of all temporal interests of man–property, reputation, the peace of all families, the arbitrations and peace of nations, liberty, life even, and the very foundations of society."[40] It is from this mold that Lincoln was formed. Burke understood the interplay of legal training and political practice. Lincoln's life perfected the mold. There is much evidence for celebrating Lincoln as a triumphant war leader. Certainly he was more effective in his last year than his first.

---

[38] James D Horan, *The Pinkertons: The Detective Dynasty that Made History* (New York: Crown Publishers, 1967) 130-33.

[39] David Donald, *Lincoln* (New York: Simon & Schuster, 1995) 394.

[40] Edmund Burke, Ross J. S. Hoffman and Paul Levack, eds., *Burke's Politics: Selected Writings and Speeches of Edmund Burke* (New York: Alfred A. Knopf, 1949) 72.

If it were not so sad, it would be almost ludicrous, to believe that in the midst of his problems, Lincoln pored over the pages of Henry W. Halleck's translation of Jomini[41] while his capital was asleep. And what was the result? In 1864, when Grant was appointed to command the armies, he said, "I neither ask nor desire to know anything of your plans. Take the responsibility and act, and call on me for assistance."[42] He had learned in his lawyer-like way that no man is a born strategist.

What made Lincoln a successful commander-in-chief was his constitutional "bending" within the framework of his wise, honest, restrained, inspirational temperament. Lincoln the lawyer-president avoided narrow overemphasis, and understood the difference between distortion and clarification for a higher purpose–that of preserving the Union as the greatest legal framework ever devised. As chief magistrate and commander-in-chief, Lincoln alternately encouraged the American people and ordered arms to fulfill the true destiny of the Union: to achieve its promise as "the last best hope of earth." This became possible because Abraham Lincoln, first a lawyer, and then a president, combined his love of politics and law to become a statesman. Rather than limit himself as a commander-in-chief or attorney-in-chief, he used his background to deliver the greatest performance of his life in the courtroom of world opinion.

[41] Henry Wager Halleck, *Elements of Military Art and Science*, 2nd ed. (New York, 1861).
[42] Horace Porter, *Campaigning with Grant* (New York: Century Co., 1897) 26.

Figure 9. *Abraham Lincoln* oil painting by James Montgomery Flagg. His political-legal training afforded great human insight and allowed time to ruminate about larger policy issues. (Courtesy of The Frank & Virginia Collection of Lincolniana.)

2

"THAT ATTRACTIVE RAINBOW:" THE IMAGE OF ABRAHAM LINCOLN AS COMMANDER-IN-CHIEF

By Harold Holzer

"Of all the men about Washington," the *Chicago Tribune* proclaimed during one of the bleakest hours of the Union war effort, "the best fitted to take command of the army" was Abraham Lincoln, who would later be depicted by London *Punch*, appropriately enough, as the God of War (**Figure 1**).[1]

According to the *Tribune*, the reasons were abundant. Lincoln understood more about strategy than any of his advisors, "civil or military." If only his instructions to his generals had been had followed, the rebel army would long ago have been "cut to pieces and destroyed, and the war virtually ended." He even knew the terrain—"every path, road, defile, mountain, stream and wood." The *Tribune* therefore urged "that Old Abe take the reins into his own hands." As "President, General-in-Chief, and Secretary of War in one," he would surely "lead our armies to victory."[2]

But few Northerners, civil or military, joined the bandwagon. Heard far more often than endorsements of the *Tribune's* call to arms were charges that the president had already

---

[1] London *Punch*, 25 March 1865.
[2] Herbert Mitgang, ed., *Lincoln as They Saw Him* (New York: Rinehart & Co., 1956) 343-44.

VULCAN IN THE SULKS.

BRITANNIA. "IF YOU TURN SULKY, AND WON'T MAKE MY ARMOUR, HOW SHALL I BE ABLE TO RESIST MARS?"

Figure 1. John Tenniel, *Vulcan in the Sulks*. Wood engraving published in *Punch*, or the *London Charivari*, 25 March 1865. The print warns of an imagined American military threat to Britain, portraying Lincoln as Mars, the Roman god of war. (Photo: The Punch Library, London)

assumed far too much power: nothing short of "despotism" and "absolutism" in the words of the *New York Daily News*.[3]

Union men had other reasons to doubt Lincoln's ability to lead troops, even after formally trained commanders like Ambrose P. Burnside and Joseph Hooker failed miserably on the battlefield. By the time the *Tribune* issued its call, Northern civilians had for three long years been inundated with popular prints—pictures made to be displayed in family homes—that suggested in the strongest graphic terms that Abraham Lincoln was in fact the quintessential civilian.

Such an image emphasis was understandable. Amid charges of dictatorship fueled by Lincoln's extraordinary executive actions—suspending habeas corpus, introducing the nation's first military draft (one cartoonist portrayed him as an insatiable warrior in an armored skirt, swallowing new enlistees whole), and proclaiming emancipation for slaves in the rebel states— many Northerners needed reassurance that Lincoln was not assuming vast and unprecedented new powers. During the Civil War, Lincoln prints provided just such reassurance. Most portrayed Lincoln not as a soldier but as a statesman.

The man whom many newspapers labeled a tyrant seemed in scores of period pictures the model of civilian restraint—at least, for a while. Eventually, he was portrayed as a commander-in-chief, but it took at least two years for such tributes to begin in earnest. They might well have appeared sooner, but for the fact that Lincoln suffered from a stubborn image problem that he brought on himself during the journey to his inauguration: the image of a coward. Printmakers did not routinely issue commander-in-chief prints depicting Lincoln until three major events occurred that were momentous enough to correct his early image of cowardice: First, Lincoln issued the Emancipation Proclamation; second, Lincoln sought re-election in 1864 as the war candidate against a Peace Democrat; and third, he was assassinated, becoming, in a sense, the last casualty of the Rebellion.

[3] Ibid., 371, 379.

Popular prints of the period vividly recall the evolution of the military aspect of Lincoln's image. It is important to remember that the images were produced by commercial publishers, not political artists-for-hire. They are not mere illustrations, though they often turn up as such today in magazines and books. In their time, proudly displayed by their owners, they reflected public sentiment about Abraham Lincoln. And, in a way, they may have reflected as well Abraham Lincoln's own sentiments about himself. For as president, Lincoln occasionally entertained the idea of taking to the field. Throughout his adult life, in fact, he seemed to harbor deep ambivalence about the allure of military distinction.

Back in 1832, while still a young man living in New Salem, Lincoln enlisted to fight in the Black Hawk War, and to his "surprize [sic]," was promptly elected captain of his company by his fellow volunteers. "No success before or after, he admitted, ever gave him "so much satisfaction."[4]

But Lincoln harbored no illusions about his subsequent war service, the only time he spent in uniform. He never saw any Indians, he confessed, "but I had a good many bloody struggles with the musquetoes [sic]." In a more reflective moment, Lincoln worried profoundly about the hypnotic allure of military glory, "that attractive rainbow, that rises in showers of blood — that serpent's eye, that charms to destroy." Later, as Congressman, he opposed the Mexican War, and paid a heavy political price: he was out of elective office for years.[5]

When he sought a comeback by running for the Senate in 1858, his opponent, Stephen A. Douglas reminded voters that Lincoln had "distinguished himself" in the House of Representatives "by taking the side of the common enemy, in time of war, against his own country." Lincoln lost the Senate race, but two years later won the Republican nomination for president. In a sense, he was thus exonerated for his early opposition to

---

[4] Roy P. Basler et al, eds., *The Collected Works of Abraham Lincoln* (hereafter referred to as *Collected Works*), 4:8 (New Brunswick NJ: Rutgers University Press, 1953-1955) 64.

[5] Ibid., 1:8, 509-10; Gabor S. Boritt, ed., *Lincoln the War President: The Gettysburg Lectures* (New York: Oxford University Press, 1992) xxvii.

American military glory, at least by party leaders casting votes at the Republican National Convention of 1860. To ordinary American voters outside Illinois, however, he remained virtually unknown. Print portraits would introduce him to America that year, and provide biographical context as well.[6]

Many printmakers responded by stressing Lincolnian attributes that were physical, though decidedly civilian. In prints showing him as a railsplitter and flatboatman, Lincoln was portrayed as an American success story who escaped frontier poverty by sweat and strength. Even in caricature that mocked him, reminders of his strenuous life were much in evidence. He might be depicted as a baseball player, swinging with a railsplitter's maul, as a tight-rope walker making his way across troubled waters, or as a gymnast desperate for a boost to avoid being split in two by his own log rails. When the race was reduced in graphic terms to a boxing match, there could be little doubt that the legendary wrestling champion was destined to prevail.[7]

But even the prize-fighting metaphor was pugilistic, not military. Perhaps that is why even after the election, at least for one printmaker, it did not seem quite enough that Lincoln rose from log cabin to White House. The engraver added a bit of family glory by noting that Lincoln's father had been killed by Indians. The only problem was that the story was not true. Other image-makers felt Lincoln's rugged appearance suggested Jacksonian determination. Who could be more military than Old Hickory? But one artist who tried to portray him as a second Jackson earned only laughter. Lincoln was elected in spite of such portraiture.[8]

---

[6] Harold Holzer, ed., *The Lincoln-Douglas Debates: The First Complete, Unexpurgated Text* (New York: Harper Collins, 1993) 51.

[7] See, for example, the following prints by lithographers Currier & Ives of New York: *The National Game. Three "Outs" and One "Run"/Abraham Lincoln Winning the Ball; The Political Gymnasium;* and *Political "Blondins" Crossing Salt River,* in Rufus Rockwell Wilson, *Lincoln in Caricature: A Historical Collection with Descriptive and Biographical Commentary* (New York: Horizon Press, 1953) 27, 35, 37.

[8] Portrait of *President-Elect Abraham Lincoln* in *Frank Leslie's Illustrated Newspaper,* 21 November 1860; for Charles Alfred Barry's controversial, Jacksonian portrait of Lincoln, see Harold Holzer, Gabor

Thus he took the oath of office bearing neither military credentials nor a military image. Looking to his inaugural address for inspiration, artist Thomas Nast was so confused by Lincoln's vow to hold federal property in the South on the one hand—and his conciliatory "we must not be enemies...but friends" plea on the other—that he could not decide whether the new president was a man of peace or a man of war. So he portrayed him as both: one panel of his cartoon ("War") showing a fierce, armor-clad Lincoln standing over a beaten foe, bloodied sword in hand; and the other ("Peace") depicting him smiling benignly, wearing a flowing dress, and daintily holding aloft the scales of justice. Less than six weeks later, Fort Sumter was attacked, and Lincoln was suddenly commander-in-chief of a nation under attack. Unfortunately, Lincoln's preinaugural entrance into Washington had not been calculated to inspire confidence.[9]

Warned that an assassination plot awaited him in hostile Baltimore, Lincoln agreed to rush through the city by night, wearing an uncharacteristic soft hat and overcoat to avoid recognition. Thus attired, he was reported to have admitted, "I was not the same man." He arrived in Washington safely, but with his image about to be badly tarnished.[10]

Northern artists quickly exaggerated Lincoln's Baltimore disguise into a comic Scottish cap and military cape, and bombarded the illustrated weeklies with lampoons showing Lincoln cowering in fear before wholly imaginary assailants. When, months later, a Richmond-based printmaker portrayed Lincoln fleeing comically from the first, feeble Confederate cannon, he was showed him still dressed in the absurd Scotch cap and flowing cape. The Baltimore image would not easily go away.[11]

At first, printmakers mustered only tepid responses to the onslaught of "coward" pictures. One such image showed

---

S. Boritt, and Mark E. Neely, Jr., *The Lincoln Image: Abraham Lincoln and the Popular Print* (New York: Scribner's, 1984) 51-55.

[9] *Harper's Weekly*, 9 March 1861.

[10] Don E. Fehrenbacher and Virginia Fehrenbacher, eds., *Recollected Words of Lincoln* (Stanford: Stanford University Press, 1996) 306.

[11] See *The Abe-Iad*, illustrated sheet music cover published by John H. Parrott, Richmond, in Weldon Petz, *In the Presence of Abraham Lincoln* (Harrogate TN: Lincoln Memorial University, 1973) 44.

Lincoln not as soldier but sportsman (**Figure 2**), recoiling from his poorly aimed rifle shot as his target, a bird labeled "C.S.A.," thumbs his nose at the hapless hunter. Evidently, not even a gun-toting Lincoln was to be taken seriously.

Ironically, the one print that might have had an ameliorating impact on Lincoln's prevailing post-inaugural image failed to have much impact for an altogether different reason: it was never completed or distributed. On 24 May 1861 a lithographer named Carl Anton copyrighted a sketch of Lincoln holding off a bayonet-wielding Jefferson Davis with one of his signature log rails. But just a few weeks after Anton registered this optimistic design, the Union suffered a humiliating defeat at the first battle of the war, and the picture may suddenly have seemed over-optimistic. Maybe that is why it survives today only in preliminary form, its caption written hastily in ink. No finished copy has ever been found. It was apparently never formally published because its creator determined that the public would not accept it.

What is astounding is that Lincoln ultimately overcame the humiliating early images, eventually earning praise for military leadership. According to Civil War scholar T. Harry Williams, Lincoln grew into a better strategist "than any of his generals" and "did more than Grant or any general to win the war for the Union." He became, "in actuality as well as in title the commander in chief." But as Lincoln biographer David Herbert Donald has maintained, the sixteenth president came to office both "inexperienced" and "insecure" as an administrator, a military tyro who might be reading a war primer like Henry Halleck's *Elements of Military Art and Science* at the very same time he was issuing orders to professional soldiers. His own attorney general early on concluded of Lincoln, "he has not the power to command," while General George B. McClellan

Figure 2. Printmaker unknown, *The SPORTSMAN upset by the RECOIL of his own Gun.* Lithograph, ca. 1864. Lincoln's weapon bears the inscription, "To whom it may concern," probably a derisive reference to the president's memorandum, following publisher Horace Greely's failed peace mission to Canada, reaffirming the government's willingness to consider future armistice proposals. In short, the cartoon suggests that Lincoln's reconstruction plans are backfiring. (Photo: Library of Congress)

dismissed him as "an idiot," and "nothing more than a well-meaning baboon."[12]

Lincoln would prove Bates, McClellan, and his many other critics, wrong, but it would take time—in life as well as art. At the beginning of the Civil War, Lincoln still understandably seemed to most image-makers to be facing the battle of his life against his Confederate presidential counterpart, the almost wholly military Jefferson Davis.

Like Lincoln, Davis had fought in the Black Hawk War, but there the pre-presidential résumés sharply diverged. Davis went on to West Point, and when Lincoln was fighting against the Mexican War, Davis was fighting in it. Davis even served before the Rebellion as the nation's secretary of war. Most Northern image-makers immediately understood the differences between America's two Civil War presidents.

In New York, for example, before secession made it impossible to export such pictures to Southern audiences, one lithographer issued a print not only showing Davis alongside Generals Robert E. Lee, Joseph E. Johnston, "Stonewall" Jackson and others—but like them, garbed in full military uniform. Later, inspired by rumors—false, as it turned out—that Davis appeared at Bull Run in uniform to rally his troops there to victory, a Richmond lithographer issued a best-selling portrait of Davis on horseback, riding dramatically onto the battlefield to lead the army.[13]

Lincoln could not hope to compete with such powerful martial imagery, even if it was undeserved. The best that prints could do was show him in early councils of war. One example (**Figure 3**) managed to make "Old Fuss and Feathers," Winfield

---

[12] T. Harry Williams, *Lincoln and His Generals* (New York: Alfred A. Knopf, 1952) vii; David Herbert Donald, *Lincoln* (New York: Simon & Schuster, 1996) 285, 329; Howard K. Beale, ed., *The Diary of Edward Bates...* (Washington, DC: US Government Printing Office, 1933) 220; Stephen Sears, ed., *The Civil War Papers of George B. McClellan: Selected Correspondence 1860-1865* (New York: Ticknor & Fields, 1989) 85, 106.
[13] Mark E. Neely, Jr., Harold Holzer, and Gabor S. Boritt, *The Confederate Image: Prints of the Lost Cause* (Chapel Hill: University of North Carolina Press 1987) 15-19.

Figure 3. [Robert] Whitechurch after Christian Schussele, *President Lincoln and His Cabinet, with Lt Genl Scott/In the Council Chamber at the White House.* Steel engraving, Philadelphia, circa 1861. Such prints, portraying Lincoln chairing war councils, were designed to reassure Union audiences that the military was being well-managed. The artist who sketched this scene probably visited Lincoln's Executive Mansion office, because he produced a realistic-looking impression of the room. (Photo: Harold Holzer)

Scott, look younger—but did little to make the seated Lincoln seem very commanding. Another, equally unconvincing, print added George B. McClellan, John C. Frémont, Robert Anderson, and others to the conference table—generals who in life were no more likely to gather together in the same room than Lincoln and Davis.

Even though such pictures suggested harmony in pursuing strategy, they could hardly promote the notion that Lincoln, in his familiar swallow-tail coat, white shirt, and tie, was anything but the nation's representative civilian magistrate. "Black coats are at a discount in the presence of the blue," Lincoln admitted, "and I recognize the merit of the discount." But trading black for blue was something Lincoln could not do.[14]

Attempts to crown Lincoln with allegorical glory seemed equally ill-advised. Artist David Gilmour Blythe's painting of *Lincoln Crushing the Dragon of Secession*, for example, depicted a president wearing neither uniform nor formal mufti, but in homespun clothing suggestive of his prairie days. Not surprisingly, the canvas was never copied for a popular print. Another symbolic effort, *The Outbreak of Rebellion*, faced different problems. The lithograph somehow suggested that Lincoln's spent the early days of the war fighting money-mad Northern capitalists, not Southern secessionists.[15]

Lincoln could hardly live up to such grandiose imagery. What he did instead was make every effort to show support for his soldiers—doffing his hat to regiments as they marched past the White House, or traveling to the front to review troops in person, often to "thunderous applause."[16]

Not everyone appreciated such appearances. One critic was emboldened to inform the president bluntly that "soldiers write home to their friends...with reference to their disappointment in

[14] Fehrenbacher and Fehrenbacher, ed., *Recollected Words of Lincoln*, 126.
[15] For Blythe, see Harold Holzer and Mark E. Neely, Jr., *Mine Eyes Have Seen the Glory: The Civil War in Art* (New York: Orion Books, 1993) 82-83; for Kimmel and Forster's print, *The Outbreak of the Rebellion*, see Holzer, Boritt, and Neely, *Lincoln Image*, 85.
[16] See Harold Holzer, "Lincoln at the Front: Abraham Lincoln Visits the Battlefields of the Civil War," *Blue & Gray Magazine* I (February-March 1984): 50.

your bearing and manners when reviewing them." Explained the angry author: "They say when you are on horseback, and platoons of men marching by you, that you lean about and turn your head to talk with people behind you, when...you should sit erect and talk to nobody and look straight at the saluting soldiers—that you ought to assume some dignity for the occasion even though your breeding has not been military." The president's bad form, the outspoken correspondent added, "don't require half so much sacrifice on your part to rectify as it does of the men to go from their homes for the hardship they undertake.... For God's sake consult...some military man, as to what you ought to do on these occasions in military presence."[17]

Much to Lincoln's benefit, such occasions, however undignified they looked to some, were usually sketched sympathetically by the "special artists" covering the war for the widely read illustrated newspapers. Alfred R. Waud, for one, drew Lincoln reviewing a New Jersey brigade at the White House in 1861 (**Figure 4**). And when Lincoln visited Hooker's army on 9 April 1863, Waud was there once again to provide a drawing for the picture press. Such confirmation of Lincoln's presence among his troops could doubtless be comforting during the darker days of the Union war effort—not only to the troops he visited, but to those on the home front who saw the pictorial reports.[18]

On another such occasion, for example, photographer Alexander Gardner was on hand to record Lincoln's visit to McClellan after the Battle of Antietam. Gardner posed the tall president and his diminutive field commander face-to-face in several famous poses. In revealing the contrast in height between general and president, Gardner provided a perhaps unintended, but powerful, reminder of the dominance of civilian authority. To suggest the rough life on campaign, he also photographed Lincoln and McClellan meeting inside a tent. Modern viewers who have seen the uncropped original photos

[17] Robert Colby to Abraham Lincoln, 18 May 1861, Abraham Lincoln Papers, Library of Congress.
[18] Original drawings in the Prints & Photographs Division, Library of Congress.

Figure 4. Printmaker unknown, after Alfred Waud, *The New Jersey brigade passing in review before the President*. Published in the *New-York Illustrated News*, 25 May 1861. Lincoln reviews the troops alongside his wife and one of his sons, in a print that may have been designed to suggest united family support for the war effort, in the wake of rumors of Mary Lincoln's disloyalty. (Photo: Library of Congress)

know that directly behind these tents stood a large house. So the two could easily have met in more comfortable surroundings, but not without sacrificing an irresistible photo opportunity.[19]

Understandably, however, neither newspaper woodcuts nor photographs exerted the same emotional impact on American audiences as popular prints designed for permanent display in that most sacred of all domestic settings, the wall above the family hearth. And these still, stubbornly, failed to acknowledge Lincoln's growing military authority.

Ironically, Lincoln's image seemed least military around the time he probably most yearned to fulfill the *Chicago Tribune*'s wish that he take personal command. In May 1862, he cruised to Hampton Roads, Virginia, and for a time actually assumed direct control of a Union action against Norfolk. Secretary of the Treasury Salmon P. Chase, no great admirer, was moved to admit in his diary: "I think it quite certain that if he had not come down, [Norfolk] would still have been in possession of the enemy." But no artist was on hand to record Lincoln's triumph. A drawing by Charles Reinhart showing Lincoln plotting tactics on board ship with Secretary of War Edwin M. Stanton, Secretary of the Treasury Salmon P. Chase, and General Egbert Viele was not made until years later, for a Lincoln biography written by his onetime private secretary.[20]

Once tested in action at Norfolk, Lincoln became less tolerant about "procrastination on the part of commanders." Even military successes did not ease Lincoln's frustration. "After every small victory," he complained, "I am crowded by men of every rank from a colonel down to a corporal, each one claiming the honor to themselves...and of course demanding a promotion." Once, after learning that Confederate raiders had seized a Union general and twelve mules, Lincoln is reported to have

[19] Charles Hamilton and Lloyd Ostendorf, *Lincoln in Photographs: An Album of Every Known Pose*, Rev. ed. (Dayton OH: Morningside Books, 1985) 107.
[20] David Donald, ed., *Inside Lincoln's Cabinet: The Civil War Diaries of Salmon P. Chase* (New York: Longmans, Green & Co., 1954) 85; for Reinhart see William O. Stoddard, *Abraham Lincoln: The True Story of a Great Life*, Rev. ed. (New York: Fords, Howard & Hulbert, 1896) opp. 210.

sneered uncharacteristically: "How unfortunate; I can fill his place with one of my generals in five minutes, but those mules cost us two hundred dollars apiece."[21]

He remained a divided man. Part of him believed, as he told Hooker, that "you do not mix politics with your profession." But he knew all too well that "defeat and failure in the field make everything seem wrong." So part of him still yearned to take up arms. "How willingly would I exchange places," he confessed, "...with the soldier who sleeps on the ground in the Army of the Potomac." When that army failed to follow its victory at Gettysburg with the pursuit he believed could have ended the war, Lincoln exploded: "If I had gone up there I could have whipped them myself." He confided to one contemporary that soon he "must take these army matters into his own hands."[22]

Prints of the day still did not pave the way for such a transfiguration. Even an image praising the government for resisting threats of British intervention assigned the credit to only a representative Uncle Sam (**Figure 5**). What did offer promise to Lincoln's iconographical future is the change in that old symbol. For years, depictions of the "Uncle Sam" character had made that national symbol look like the Father of his Country (**Figure 6**). Now he suddenly resembled Father Abraham.

Lincoln's only subsequent exposure to combat did not come until the summer of 1864, when Jubal Early's troops threatened Washington. Lincoln rode out to the scene of the action at Fort Stevens. Climbing onto a parapet, his tall stovepipe hat an easy

---

[21] Fehrenbacher and Fehrenbacher, ed., *Recollected Words of Lincoln*, 113, 200; Mark E. Neely, Jr., "Wilderness and the Cult of Manliness: Hooker, Lincoln, and Defeat," in Gabor S. Boritt, ed., *Lincoln's Generals* (New York: Oxford University Press, 1994) 65.

[22] Basler, ed., *Collected Works*, 4:78; Donald, *Lincoln*, 429; James M. McPherson, "Lincoln and the Strategy of Unconditional Surrender," in *Lincoln the War President*, ed. Boritt, 46; Fehrenbacher and Fehrenbacher, ed., *Recollected Words of Lincoln*, 331.

UNCLE SAM PROTECTING HIS PROPERTY AGAINST THE ENCROACHMENTS OF HIS COUSIN JOHN.

Figure 5. E. Stauch, *Uncle Sam Protecting His Property Against the Encroachments of His Cousin John*. Lithograph, Philadelphia, 1861. As he clutches a bunch of cotton, Brother Jonathan—the national symbol of Britain—is forcibly evicted from a representative American field by "Uncle Sam," in the form of a prototypical Union soldier who looks very much like Lincoln. Note the crow perched on the fence at left, intended to depict French Emperor Napoleon III, who appears frightened by the scene. (Photo: Library of Congress)

Figure 6. Currier & Ives, *"Uncle Sam" Making New Arrangements.* Lithograph, New York, 1860. As this pre-war print indicates, before the Rebellion Lincoln was most commonly portrayed as a railsplitter dressed in homespun, while the national symbol Uncle Sam (center, hand raised) bore a close resemblance instead to George Washington. (Photo: Library of Congress)

target for enemy sharpshooters, he exposed himself to enemy fire. For this display of bravery, a young officer named Oliver Wendell Holmes Jr. bellowed, "Get down you fool!"[23]

Like an echo, the image-makers still refused to portray Lincoln rising up in military glory. Few of his contemporaries ever knew that Lincoln had displayed personal courage at Fort Stevens, or that during one inspiring review of his army, he rode six miles on horseback within three hundred perilous yards of Confederate entrenchments, in full view of Rebel pickets. Urged to move his procession elsewhere, Lincoln responded: "Oh, no...the commander-in-chief...must not show any cowardice in front of his soldiers," adding softly, "however he may feel."[24]

The closest his earliest image-makers had come to creating an equestrian portrait of Lincoln was an 1860 campaign print by Currier & Ives, lampooning him as an organ-grinder's monkey, riding a hobby horse. In the more sophisticated, but equally unflattering wartime equestrian view by Adalbert Volck, a gifted pro-Confederate Baltimore artist, the best that could be said of Lincoln as president was that he was a modern version of the hapless Don Quixote, tilting at distant windmills alongside his latter-day Sancho Panza, the controversial General Benjamin F. Butler. Lincoln's wartime military image might have suffered greatly had Volck's ingenious, assaultive etchings become available to a wide public. But Volck's efforts were only published secretly, and distributed in small editions.[25] Not surprisingly, Confederate printmakers expressed particular disdain for Lincoln's military leadership, and for a time, unlike Volck, were free to air their venom. Had they possessed the skill to funnel their venom into effective graphics, Lincoln's reputation in period prints might have been gravely injured.

---

[23] Earl Schenck Miers, ed., *Lincoln Day by Day: A Chronology, 1809-1865* (Washington, DC: Lincoln Sesquicentennial Commission, 1960) 3:271-72; Jay Monaghan, *Diplomat in Carpet Slippers: Abraham Lincoln Deals With Foreign Affairs* (Indianapolis: Bobbs-Merrill Co., 1945) 378.
[24] Allen Thorndike Rice, ed., *Reminiscences of Lincoln by Distinguished Men of His Time* (New York: The Century Co., 1888) 147.
[25] See Currier & Ives, *The Great Exhibition of 1860*, in Wilson, *Lincoln in Caricature*, 51; for Volck see Neely, Holzer, and Boritt, *The Confederate Image*, 44-54.

But Confederate graphics became an early casualty of the Southern mobilization for war; the industry was all but dead by 1862. A hint of how effective such pictures might have been had they proliferated can be seen in a caustic but little-seen print from the ill-fated Richmond weekly, the *Southern Illustrated News*. The woodcut (**Figure 7**) cleverly presented Lincoln as a desperate puppet-master, forced to introduce his latest doll—"Fighting Joe" Hooker—having shelved such previous failures as Burnside and McClellan.

Not that Lincoln was immune from such criticism in the North. Artist David H. Strother may have intended primarily to criticize General McClellan in his series of drawings mocking the disastrous Peninsula campaign. But showing Lincoln wheeling the reluctant general towards Richmond, or literally prodding McClellan into action at the sharp end of a bayonet, may have reminded viewers, too, that on the Virginia Peninsula, Lincoln fared no better in the role of commander-in-chief than did McClellan in his as field general.[26]

A good deal of the pictorial indifference to Lincoln's military leadership finally ended on 1 January 1863, the day Lincoln unleashed the most powerful weapon of the entire war: the Emancipation Proclamation. Rejecting recommendations that he place the order "upon high moral grounds," Lincoln crafted the document "as a war measure from the Commander-in-Chief."[27]

Printmakers immediately embraced a similar approach. They sold their pictures primarily to the same white Americans to whom Lincoln framed the proclamation as a military, not a moral, instrument. Thus, it was in their interest as well to portray Emancipation as a war measure, rather than an abolitionist decree, in order to make their pictorial commemorations more attractive to mainstream white buyers. Of all the familiar images of Lincoln personally liberating grateful slaves

---

[26] For examples of Strother's works, including *A Practical Reminder*, see Stefan Lorant, *Lincoln: A Picture Story of His Life*, Rev. ed. (New York; W. W. Norton, 1969) 182.

[27] La Wanda Cox, *Lincoln and Black Freedom* (Columbia: University of South Carolina Press, 1981) 13.

THE SOUTHERN ILLUSTRATED NEWS.

MASTER ABRAHAM LINCOLN GETS A NEW TOY.

Figure 7. Printmaker unknown, *Master Abraham Gets a New Toy*. Wood engraving, published in the *Southern Illustrated News*, Richmond, 28 February 1863. With earlier, unsuccessful puppets discarded—failed Generals Scott, McDowell, Fremont, Banks, Pope, Burnside, and McClellan—toymaster Lincoln introduces "Fighting Joe" Hooker as his latest attraction. Apparently, two years after Lincoln's inauguration, the printmaker who crafted this cartoon still did not know that his subject had grown a beard. (Photo: Rare Books Division, The New York Public Library, Astor, Lenox and Tilden Foundations)

—most known to modern Americans from illustrations in history books—not one was issued while the war still raged. They were, rather, products of the period following Lincoln's assassination, when his life's work was reinterpreted in the warm glow of universal reverence.[28]

As long as he lived, Lincoln's commander-in-chief image continued to be subject to attack. Among the viciously anti-Lincoln graphics that abounded during his 1864 campaign for re-election, none was more brutal than *The Commander-in-Chief Conciliating the Soldier's Votes on the Battle Field* (**Figure 8**). The print illustrated the libel that a callous Lincoln had called for comic songs as he walked among the dead and wounded at Antietam. Another print of the period held Lincoln personally responsible for all 500,000 Union casualties to date, and made him seem ghoulishly insensitive by reacting to the death toll with another funny story.

But something else happened that election year, and it became factor two in the metamorphosis of Lincoln's military image: the nomination of George B. McClellan as his opponent for president, a former field commander now incongruously running for commander-in-chief on a peace platform. Suddenly, printmakers found it inviting to portray McClellan, not Lincoln, as a coward, lampooning the general for allegedly watching the disastrous Battle of Malvern Hill from the safety of a distant gunboat, or suggesting that as president he might collaborate with Jefferson Davis to return free blacks, even military veterans, to slavery.[29]

In this highly charged atmosphere it became just as natural for image-makers to present Lincoln, convincingly armed with a bayonet, personally repelling the threat to liberty that

---

[28] See Currier & Ives's *Freedom to the Slaves...*, in the Holzer, Boritt, and Neely, *Lincoln Image*, 102.

[29] See, for example, Currier & Ives, *The Old Bull Dog on the Right Track*, original lithograph cartoon in the Lincoln Museum, Fort Wayne IN; and Currier & Ives, *The Gunboat Candidate at the Battle of Malvern Hill*, in Bernard F. Reilly, Jr., *American Political Prints, 1766-1876: A Catalog of the Collections in the Library of Congress* (Boston: G. K. Hall, 1991) 526.

Figure 8. Printmaker unknown, *The COMMANDER-IN-CHIEF conciliating the SOLDIER'S VOTES on the Battle Field*. Lithograph, circa 1864. Indifferent to the suffering of wounded soldiers at Antietam, Lincoln asks a horrified aide to serenade him with a comic song. Lincoln holds a scotch cap, a reference to the disguise he allegedly wore in fleeing Baltimore in 1861. The compassionate officer tending to the injured man at right bears a close resemblance, surely intentional, to Lincoln's 1864 opponent for the White House, George B. McClellan. This image was crafted by the same artist responsible for the print of Lincoln the sportsman (See Figure 4). They were probably conceived as part of a series of anti-Lincoln images. (Photo: The Lincoln Museum, Fort Wayne, Indiana)

McClellan, and by complicity, Jefferson Davis himself, posed to America's future. Such prints did not totally acknowledge Lincoln as a military leader, but they moved his image closer in that direction than ever before. As a politician, he now seemed undeniably commanding, and it was a general, ironically, who made him seem so. As a French printmaker neatly put it in a telling graphic commentary on the results of the 1864 contest, Lincoln's re-election proved a military bombshell: the "rudest projectile" yet hurled by the Union against the Confederacy.[30]

Yet only after Lincoln fell victim to an assassin's bullet (the third and final factor to influence his military image) did a significant number of American graphic artists finally, fully recognize his seldom-acknowledged role as commander-in-chief. Prints commonly began showing him, together with Grant, as "Columbia's Noblest Sons," or alongside the most famous of all general-presidents, George Washington, as "founder" and "preserver" of the Union.[31]

At last, for example, Currier & Ives belatedly issued its very first council of war print, showing the president conferring, implicitly on military strategy, with Generals William T. Sherman, Philip H. Sheridan, and Ulysses S. Grant. True, even when the setting for such scenes was moved outdoors, which New York printmakers Jones & Clark did for their 1865 lithograph, *Lincoln and His Generals* (**Figure 9**). The mufti-clad president still did not seem altogether military. But at least he was now made to seem retrospectively the very center of attention, as Admirals David D. Porter and David G. Farragut, together with Generals Sherman, Grant, Sheridan, and George H. Thomas face him in rapt attention. In this celebratory marketplace for Lincoln pictures, even an instantly recognizable tribute, The *First Reading of the Emancipation Proclamation*, one of the best-selling and most influential Lincoln prints of all time,

[30] See, for example, M. W. Siebert, *Union and Liberty! Union and Slavery!*, ibid., 534; and M. Martinet, *Le plus rude projectile qu'ait encore recu le sud!*, original print from *Actualités*, in the Lincoln Museum, Fort Wayne IN.
[31] Holzer, Boritt, and Neely, *The Lincoln Image*, 193, 195.

Figure 9. Peter Kramer, *Lincoln and His Generals.* Printed by A. Brett and published by Jones & Clark, New York, circa 1865. Purporting to show a council of war on the battlefield, Lincoln is shown discussing military strategy with commanders of both his navy and army near the close of the war. The portrait of the president was modeled after the Brady photograph later engraved for the copper penny. (Photo: The Library of Congress)

could now be believably pirated and modified by a rival engraver, with the resulting composite purporting to show as a convincing scene of the late president and his cabinet in council with Grant to plan the end of the war.[32]

Perhaps the clearest signal of the posthumous improvement in Lincoln's military image came not from a print that was published, but rather one that was never issued — recalling printmaker Carl Anton's similarly abandoned effort four years earlier. Anton had believed that audiences would not accept an image of Lincoln making war. Much had changed. In 1865, it seemed unlikely that audiences would accept an image of Lincoln making peace.

On 2 February 1865, Lincoln had gone to Hampton Roads, for a secret peace conference with Confederate Vice President Stephens. The meeting failed, but that did not prevent engraver J. C. Buttre from sensing its historical importance. He began work on a print he tentatively called *Lincoln & Stephens in Hampton Roads*. Had it been polished and issued to the public, it might have become one of the most realistic of all group portraits of Lincoln, showing him presiding over a genuine "Council of Peace" in an effort to end the war. It was not to be. By the time Buttre finished work on the print, the peace initiative had collapsed, Grant had overpowered Lee, and Lincoln was dead. Suddenly, it no longer seemed appropriate to portray the martyr as anything less than tough, resolute, and at least somewhat military — an integral part of the action as the war drew to a close. Buttre never finished his proof print, and only one copy of the rough first impression has ever been found. Martyrdom effectively inoculated Lincoln against charges, verbal or visual, that he was a timid warrior.[33]

Instead, it was the wholly imaginary outdoor war council that now seemed realistic enough to inspire at least one

[32] See Thomas Kelly's 1866 lithograph, *President Lincoln and His Cabinet. with General Grant in the Council Chamber of the Whitehouse* [sic], in Harold Holzer, Gabor S. Boritt, and Mark E. Neely, Jr., *Changing the Lincoln Image* (Fort Wayne, IN: Louis A. Warren Lincoln Library and Museum, 1985) 19.

[33] Ibid., 65-67.

photographer to copy Jones & Clark's print of Lincoln and his generals (**Figure 9**), re-title it *Lincoln and His Generals in Council Before Richmond*, and issue the result as a carte-de-visite that suggested that Lincoln had personally devised the strategy that led to the capture of the Confederate capital.

Actually, Lincoln was quite close to the scene of that Union triumph. On 23 March 1865, he took the steamer River Queen to visit Grant's headquarters at City Point. He stayed for more than two weeks, his longest and last trip to the front. One of its most famous moments came on 27 March, when Grant, Sherman, and Porter boarded the ship for a final strategy meeting. It was by all accounts a war council, at which Lincoln pressed his commanders to fight on to a speedy victory. As Lincoln maintained, the "great lesson of peace" came from "teaching...all the folly of being the beginners of a war."[34]

But when painter G. P. A. Healy decided to immortalize the scene three years later, he entitled his canvas *The Peacemakers*, going so far as to insert a symbolic rainbow bursting forth outside the ship's windows. The shift in focus in what otherwise might have been the most potent of all commander-in-chief images of Lincoln was likely attributable to the artist's friendship with Sherman. It was Sherman who advised Healy on the composition, convinced Grant to pose, and got Porter to furnish details about the boat. Perhaps in return for all his help, Healy's painting showed Sherman doing the talking, as the others, including Lincoln, look on in deep thought. Whatever its shortcomings, the result inspired a chromolithograph designed for home display. But the relative scarcity of surviving copies strongly suggests that in its day it was not popular. By the time it was issued, American audiences may well have preferred images that did not stress Lincoln's efforts at conciliation.[35]

A German, not an American, lithographer may have come closest to satisfying post-assassination public taste with a highly romanticized picture of commander Lincoln, now looking

---

[34] Miers, ed., *Lincoln Day by Day*, 3:321-327; Basler, ed., *Collected Works*, 4:439.
[35] Holzer and Neely, *Mine Eyes Have Seen the Glory*, ,156.

positively warlike on horseback, riding triumphantly into City Point. The problem was, Lincoln surely never did so in real life. City Point was a bustling Union supply center, not a bombed-out ruin, as this image suggested. Wounded soldiers did not crowd its streets, and ex-slaves did not celebrate Lincoln's arrival there. Apparently, the distant European printmaker simply mistook City Point for Richmond. In so doing, he had ironically created the kind of heroic equestrian picture with which Lincoln was never honored in life. But he altogether missed the opportunity to suggest accurately the quiet entrance that Lincoln ultimately made into conquered Richmond on 4 April.[36]

Artist Dennis Malone Carter painted that event in 1866, portraying Lincoln in a grand carriage being greeted by black and white residents alike. The president indeed took such a ride in the occupied capital, but he was not greeted with equal enthusiasm by residents of both races. In fact, the white people aware of his visit responded, in the words of an eyewitness, with only "sullen, glazed stares...as if it was a disgusting sight."[37]

Far more moving—in its utter simplicity—was the moment, a few hours before this carriage tour, when Lincoln first stepped unannounced from a small boat onto the shores of the city. For a time, he walked in eerie silence. Then, a black woman suddenly recognized Lincoln. With shouts of "Glory, glory, glory," the newly liberated slave joyously heralded the arrival of the Great Emancipator, in a scene beautifully captured by engraver Benjamin B. Russell (**Figure 10**). Within minutes he was surrounded by a crush of African-American well-wishers. "Such wild, indescribable joy I never witnessed," wrote a newspaperman on the scene. "It was the great deliverer,

[36] Harold Holzer, *The Mirror Image of Civil War Memory: Abraham Lincoln and Jefferson Davis in Popular Prints*, Seventeenth Annual R. Gerald McMurtry Lecture (Fort Wayne, IN: Lincoln Museum, 1997) 32-34.

[37] John S. Barnes, "With Lincoln from Washington to Richmond in 1865," *Appleton's Magazine* 11 (June 1907): 515-24; 742-51; Harold Holzer, "I Myself Was at the Front," *Civil War Times Illustrated* 29 (January/February 1991): 34-35.

Figure 10. Benjamin B. Russell, *Lincoln Entering Richmond*. Engraving, Boston, 1865. Escorted by only a small retinue of armed troops, Lincoln and his son, Tad, make their way toward Jefferson Davis' abandoned executive mansion in Richmond on 4 April 1865. The print beautifully evoked the modest nature of the victorious commander-in-chief's entrance into the conquered Confederate capital. (Photo: Library of Congress)

meeting the delivered." Tears came to Lincoln's eyes as he made his way through the crowd, looking for all the world not like a commander-in-chief, but "a private citizen."[38]

One eyewitness quickly grasped the meaning of this, Lincoln's last and greatest military moment: "He came not as a conqueror, not with bitterness in his heart, but with kindness. He came as a friend, to alleviate sorrow and suffering—to rebuild what had been destroyed." The man of war had finally won enough battles to become a man of peace. And blessed indeed—in popular prints and in history alike—are conquering heroes who become peacemakers.[39]

[38] Holzer, "Lincoln at the Front," 54.
[39] Ibid.

3

LINCOLN AND HALLECK

By John Y. Simon

President Abraham Lincoln's appointment of Major General Henry W. Halleck as general-in-chief might rank as one of the most outstanding blunders of the Civil War. Within weeks of his arrival in Washington, Halleck had thoroughly demonstrated his incapacity for the position. Lincoln retained Halleck in office for the remainder of the Civil War nonetheless, despite constant condemnation by generals in the field and the scorn of political leaders. "Of all men whom I have encountered in high position, Halleck was the most hopelessly stupid," wrote Gen. George McClellan. "I do not think he ever had a correct military idea from beginning to end."[1] Secretary of the Treasury Salmon Chase thought that Halleck "was good for nothing, and everybody knew it except the President."[2] Halleck had obvious weaknesses. He evaded responsibility, provoked quarrels unnecessarily, and truckled to political power. Why did Lincoln retain his services in Washington?

When Lincoln assumed office, General Winfield Scott served as general-in-chief, as he had for twenty years. Now seventy-five years old, Scott was too heavy to mount a horse and too old to remain awake throughout important meetings. A hero of the War of 1812 and again a hero for his brilliant campaign in Mexico, Scott recognized his current limitations. Although a

[1] George B. McClellan, *McClellan's Own Story* (New York: Charles L. Webster, 1887) 137.
[2] 15 July 1863, *Diary of Gideon Welles: Secretary of the Navy Under Lincoln and Johnson*, Howard K. Beale, ed. (New York: W. W. Norton, 1960) 1:373.

HENRY W. HALLECK
Major-General

(Courtesy of *The Abraham Lincoln Museum*)

Virginian, Scott maintained a sturdy Unionism, attempted to retain Robert E. Lee in the Union army, and offered Lincoln seasoned advice on military matters. His unique knowledge of the talent of the old army enabled him to provide sound suggestions about potential commanders. Scott early devised an overall wartime strategy, known as the "Anaconda Plan" to defeat the Confederacy by maintaining constant pressure on all points of the enemy perimeter, including a blockade, then bisecting the South by a campaign down the Mississippi River. Scott's plan was ridiculed by those who anticipated a quick and glorious victory over the rebellion. In retrospect, however, Scott's plan closely resembles the blueprint eventually followed to Northern victory. Conscious of the burdens of age, and aware that Congress had pointedly provided the first military retirement plan in American history, Scott recommended Henry Halleck as his replacement.[3]

Halleck seemed a perfect choice. At age forty-six, he was neither immature nor overage for such weighty responsibilities. He had achieved his military reputation and standing through his own merits and hard work. He had been born to a poor farm family in upstate New York and had run away from home to escape a life of rural drudgery. Aided by a sympathetic grandfather, he had acquired an academy education and eventually an appointment to West Point. There he flourished, graduating third in his class. He began to teach chemistry at the military academy even before graduation and remained to teach engineering. As a young officer, he received choice assignments in Washington, to the fortifications in New York Harbor, and finally to a tour of inspection in Europe. Following his return from Europe, he published a book on coast defense that led to an invitation to lecture at the Lowell Institute of Boston. His lectures grew into a book, *Elements of Military Art*

---

[3] Winfield Scott to Simon Cameron, 4 October 1861, *The War of the Rebellion: A Compilation of the Official Records of the Union and Confederate Armies* (hereinafter *Official Records*) (Washington, DC: US Government Printing Office, 1880-1901) Ser. I, vol. 51, pt. 1, 491-93; T. Harry Williams, *Lincoln and His Generals* (New York: Alfred A. Knopf, 1952) 43.

and Science, first published in 1846, then reprinted, revised and enlarged, in 1861.[4]

In his book, Halleck advocated the merits of professional soldiers. He reminded readers of George Washington's complaints about the militia and his use of trained foreigners to win the Revolutionary War. War was not, Halleck argued, "a mere game of chance. Its principles constitute one of the most intricate of modern sciences; and the general who understands the art of rightly applying its rules...may be morally certain of success." For the troops, skill and discipline rather than numbers represented the formula for victory. Recognizing that Americans would fund only a small army, Halleck emphasized the education of engineer and artillery officers, those most difficult to prepare in wartime, and the training of all officers, no matter how few troops they commanded, to lead larger forces in wartime.[5] Halleck advocated a strategic offensive as the path to success. Little wonder, then, that this author appeared to be the ideal officer to take command of the U.S. Army.

Halleck was assigned to California at the outbreak of the Mexican War. Fellow officers played cards to kill time during the seven-month voyage around the tip of South America while Halleck translated four thick volumes of Jomini's life of Napoleon.[6] In California, Halleck was appointed secretary of state, translated complex Spanish land laws, initiated the movement for statehood, and wrote most of the new constitution. Even while remaining in the army, Halleck became the senior partner in Halleck, Peachy, and Billings, the leading law firm in San Francisco. He resigned from the army in 1854 with the rank of captain, effective the day after the resignation of Captain Ulysses Grant. Younger officers blocked from promo-

[4] James Grant Wilson, "General Halleck—A Memoir," *Journal of the Military Service Institution of the United States* 36 (1905): 537-41; Stephen E. Ambrose, *Halleck: Lincoln's Chief of Staff* (Baton Rouge: Louisiana State University Press, 1962) 5-7.
[5] Russell F. Weigley, *Towards an American Army: Military Thought from Washington to Marshall* (New York and London: Columbia University Press) 57-67.
[6] George W. Cullum, *Biographical Register of the Officers and Graduates of the US Military Academy...*, 3rd ed. (Boston and New York: Houghton, Mifflin, 1891) 1:735; Lloyd Lewis, *Sherman: Fighting Prophet* (New York: Harcourt, Brace, 1932) 75.

tion by a stagnant seniority system frequently resigned in frustration, some to pursue promising alternatives. Unlike Grant, who planned to start over again as a farmer, Halleck went straight to a lucrative legal career, enhanced by his mastery of Spanish land law. During seven civilian years, he had declined a professorship at the Lawrence Scientific School of Harvard, was elected president of the largest mercury mine in the country, served as a railroad president, declined an appointment to the state supreme court, and rejected overtures for a U.S. Senate seat. In his spare time, he wrote a lengthy treatise on international law, published in 1861.[7]

Scott chose Halleck as his successor because of his dazzling accomplishments in military and civilian life. Besides, Scott was under heavy pressure from General George McClellan, selected to command troops in the field when Scott could not. After Irvin McDowell, first in that role, had suffered defeat at Bull Run, McClellan was summoned from western Virginia to train and organize the forces around Washington, now named the Army of the Potomac.

McClellan soon quarreled with Scott, whom he privately denounced as "a perfect imbecile. He understands nothing, appreciates nothing is ever in my way."[8] McClellan—of all people—claimed that Scott was "for inaction & the defensive."[9] McClellan refused to forward reports through the "dotard," as he called Scott. For his part, Scott noted that the "remedy of arrest and trial before a court-martial would probably soon cure the evil," although such a trial would be "encouraging to the enemies and depressing to the friends of the Union." Consequently, wrote Scott, "I shall try to hold out" until Halleck reached Washington.[10]

---

[7] Milton H. Shutes, "Henry Wager Halleck: Lincoln's Chief of Staff," *California Historical Society Quarterly* 16 (1937): 196-200; Ambrose, *Halleck*, 7-8.

[8] McClellan to Mary Ellen McClellan, 8 August 1861, *The Civil War Papers of George B. McClellan: Selected Correspondence, 1860-65*, ed. Stephen W. Sears, (New York: Ticknor & Fields, 1989) 81.

[9] McClellan to Mary Ellen McClellan, 13 October 1861, ibid., 107.

[10] Scott to Simon Cameron, 4 October 1861, *Congressional Globe*, 37th Cong., 3rd Sess., 1263.

George B. McClellan
(Courtesy of *The Abraham Lincoln Museum*)

When urged to advance, McClellan had offered a series of excuses, some involving blame placed on Scott. When Lincoln's close friend, Edward D. Baker, lost his life while blundering into unnecessary and humiliating defeat at Ball's Bluff, McClellan increased his complaints about Scott, who was soon hustled off to retirement at West Point even before his intended successor could complete his lengthy journey from California. In his message to Congress one month later, Lincoln announced McClellan's appointment, noting that "the retiring chief repeatedly expressed his judgment in favor of General McClellan," an incredible misrepresentation abetted by Scott's patriotic refusal to publicize his contempt for his successor.[11]

Halleck arrived in Washington to find McClellan holding the position of general-in-chief. McClellan immediately ordered Halleck to command the Western Department, recently mishandled for one hundred days by General John C. Frémont. Halleck arrived in St. Louis on 19 November determined to eliminate corruption, to institute sound military procedure, and to rid Missouri of armed rebels. Halleck had never commanded troops and had no inclination to leave his desk for the field. He defined his first task as concentrating troops in Missouri.

At the eastern edge of Halleck's department, at Cairo, Illinois, Brigadier General Ulysses Grant chafed at his inactivity. Already guilty of launching an attack at Belmont before Halleck could reorganize his department, Grant's initial request to attack Fort Henry was rebuffed by Halleck.[12] Wringing reluctant approval, Grant attacked successfully, then marched toward Fort Donelson while Halleck averted his eyes, ready to take credit for victory, to disclaim responsibility for defeat. Grant's victory encouraged a jubilant Halleck to request enlargement of his department and promotions for many officers beside Grant. Still distrusting his aggressive subordinate, Halleck dispatched a flurry of charges against Grant to McClellan, including one that Grant had "resumed his former habits."

[11] 3 December 1861, *The Collected Works of Abraham Lincoln*, Roy P. Basler et al., eds., (New Brunswick: Rutgers University Press, 1953-1955) 6:31.

[12] *Personal Memoirs of U. S. Grant* (New York: Charles L. Webster, 1885-1886) 1:287.

Unaware of this last charge but outraged nonetheless, Grant asked to be relieved, backing down only when Halleck portrayed himself as Grant's defender and restored him to command the Tennessee River expedition. Surprised at Shiloh, Grant more than redeemed himself in a second day of battle, but Halleck decided to take personal command of the advance on Corinth, Mississippi, assigning Grant to a meaningless role as second in command.[13]

Having united three armies, Halleck eventually occupied Corinth after a campaign notable for unnecessary caution, crowned with an opportunity for the foe to withdraw intact. With an army of 120,000 at Corinth, Halleck could have advanced in any direction. He went nowhere. While fortifying Corinth on an elaborate scale, Halleck sent Don Carlos Buell eastward to pursue the enemy with strict orders to repair the railroad as he advanced. This prevented Buell from reaching his opponents and did the railroad no good, since guerrillas destroyed track more quickly than Union troops rebuilt it.

In the meantime, McClellan had eventually moved against Richmond. As he left, Lincoln had relieved McClellan as general-in-chief and retained McDowell's Corps for the defense of Washington. With McClellan commanding the army on which rested the nation's hopes, Lincoln had firmly expressed his lack of confidence. Under the circumstances, the wonder is not that McClellan failed to take Richmond but that he came so close. Following the climactic Seven Days battles, McClellan withdrew to Harrison's Landing and refused to advance unless massively reinforced. Consistent with earlier conduct, he blamed Lincoln and Stanton for the campaign's failure. Further, in his celebrated Harrison's Landing letter, much to Lincoln's dismay, he discussed war aims rather than strategy. As Lincoln put it, McClellan "had so skillfully handled his troops in not getting to Richmond as to retain their confidence."[14] Lincoln brought John Pope to Washington to take command of forces defending the

---

[13] John Y. Simon, *Grant and Halleck: Contrasts in Command* (Milwaukee: Marquette University Press, 1996) 14-20.

[14] Gideon Welles, *Lincoln and Seward* (New York: Sheldon & Co., 1874) 197.

capitol. Pope urged Lincoln to bring Halleck to take overall command.

Late in June, Lincoln visited Scott at West Point. Scott reaffirmed his faith in Halleck, and Lincoln began a curious courtship that included sending Senator William Sprague of Rhode Island to Halleck's headquarters. Halleck telegraphed to Lincoln, "If I were to go to Washington I could advise but one thing—to place all the forces in North Carolina, Virginia, and Washington under one head, and hold that head responsible for the result."[15] The next day, Lincoln appointed Halleck general-in-chief. Desperately frustrated by McClellan's passivity at Harrison's Landing, Lincoln sought an intermediary who would force him to advance or terminate his command.

Had Lincoln known more about Halleck's command in the West, he might have hesitated before making this crucial appointment. Halleck had already displayed excessive caution, avoidance of responsibility, duplicity, petty tyranny, and military ineptitude. He excelled in managerial capacity but lacked any skill in personal relations. He placed his own welfare above all other concerns. He had, however, concealed those faults successfully. Grant, his chief victim, had welcomed Halleck to Shiloh, calling him "one of the greatest men of the age."[16] As he left for Washington, Grant called him "a man of gigantic intellect and well studied in the profession of arms. He and I have had several little spats but I like and respect him nevertheless."[17]

From Lincoln's perspective, Halleck seemed the engineer of the successful Tennessee River campaign that had carried Union arms from Cairo to Corinth. After Shiloh, he commanded the largest army ever assembled in North America. He had the respect and endorsement of Scott as well as the enthusiastic backing of Pope. In matters of military procedure, he had long been an acknowledged expert. Furthermore, Lincoln had no better candidate for general-in-chief, and to maintain that va-

[15] *Official Records.*, Ser. I, vol. 11, pt. 3, 311-12.
[16] Grant to Julia Dent Grant, 30 April 1862, *The Papers of Ulysses S. Grant*, John Y. Simon, ed. (Carbondale and Edwardsville: Southern Illinois University Press, 1967-) 5:102.
[17] Grant to Elihu B. Washburne, 22 July 1862, ibid., 226.

cancy meant direct and unprofitable contact with the hostile McClellan.

Halleck's appointment made him McClellan's superior, inverting their roles of three months earlier. Neither handled this exchange well. Halleck held the post of general-in-chief "contrary to my own wishes," he wrote to McClellan, who responded, "I would have advised your appointment," and offered "full and cordial support."[18] Privately, McClellan called Halleck's appointment a "slap in the face," and thought it "grating to have to serve under the orders of a man I know by experience to be my inferior."[19] Halleck thought McClellan a "selfish" general who "does not understand strategy and should never plan a campaign."[20] Lincoln gave Halleck authority to remove McClellan, hoping that he would use it, yet Halleck refused to take such drastic and unpopular action.

Halleck arrived in Washington at a moment of unparalleled Northern opportunity. McClellan lay idle at Harrison's Landing with more than enough men to capture Richmond while Pope had assembled troops south of Washington sufficient to defend the capital and to advance toward Richmond. Had Halleck co-ordinated a renewal of McClellan's offensive with Pope's advance, Lee could have been crushed between two mighty armies. Instead, Halleck listened to McClellan's unrealistic demands for reinforcement, decided that they could not be met, yet declined to order McClellan forward with the enormous army he already possessed. Halleck then ordered McClellan's troops back to Washington, a move that McClellan resisted and delayed. When it became clear that McClellan was withdrawing from the peninsula and that not all of his troops had joined Pope, Lee struck at Second Bull Run.

Lee's defeat of Halleck's protégé Pope brought back McClellan, whose return to power was announced in orders

[18] Halleck to McClellan, 30 July 1862, *Official Records*, Ser. I, vol. 11, pt. 3, 343; McClellan to Halleck, 1 August 1862, ibid., 345.
[19] McClellan to Mary Ellen McClellan, 20 July 1862, and McClellan to Samuel L. M. Barlow, 23 July 1862, Sears, ed., McClellan *Papers*, 368-69.
[20] Halleck to Mrs. Halleck, 4, 5, 28 July, 9 August 1862, Wilson "Halleck," 556-57.

attributed to Halleck. Lincoln had made the decision, not even informing Halleck in advance, but took every step to evade responsibility.[21] Lincoln artfully convinced his chief advisers that he had recalled McClellan to command on Halleck's advice. McClellan now felt free to express his contempt for Halleck while leading the Army of the Potomac to meet Lee's invasion of Maryland. Believing that he had won a substantial victory at Antietam, McClellan expected as his reward the removal of Halleck, "an incompetent fool," and "the most stupid idiot I ever heard of."[22] Halleck relayed to McClellan Lincoln's repeated orders to pursue the enemy. By ignoring them, McClellan achieved his final removal from command. Halleck should then have been in firm control of the army.

He did not want that. With McClellan's successor Burnside, Halleck played a game of deadly errors. Burnside proposed to move his army to Falmouth, opposite Fredericksburg, and cross the Rappahannock on pontoons. Halleck insisted that the army cross above Fredericksburg where pontoons would be unnecessary. Burnside moved to Falmouth, found that Halleck had neglected to send the pontoons, and refused to cross the river, which was then easily fordable. Instead he awaited the pontoons, giving Lee more than ample time to assemble his army and to fortify his position. Apprehensive of impending calamity, Lincoln asked Halleck to order Burnside to abandon his plans for attack. Halleck refused. He argued that a general in the field was the best judge of operations. Halleck told Lincoln that if he wanted to control Burnside, he would have to do so himself.[23] When the battle of Fredericksburg turned into inevitable disaster, Burnside accepted responsibility. Critics, however, blamed Halleck. Burnside later advocated the removal of himself, Stanton, and Halleck, all of whom had lost the nation's confidence.[24] When Burnside proposed yet another

---

[21] Halleck testimony, 7 March 1863, *Report of the Joint Committee on the Conduct of the War* (Washington, DC: US Government Printing Office, 1863) 1:451.
[22] McClellan to Mary Ellen McClellan, 20 September, 2 October 1862, McClellan *Papers*, ed. Sears, 473, 488.
[23] Ambrose, *Halleck*, 97.
[24] Williams, *Lincoln and His Generals*, 203.

move across the Rappahannock despite the doubts of corps commanders, Lincoln asked Halleck to visit the army, then submit an opinion. Halleck refused. "Your military skill is useless to me if you will not do this," wrote Lincoln.[25] In response, Halleck submitted his resignation. Lincoln endorsed his own letter: "Withdrawn, because considered harsh by Gen. Halleck." Harsh? Certainly. Justified? Absolutely. Halleck had managed to work himself into a position of virtual uselessness to the country. Lincoln's annual message of 1862, unlike that of one year earlier that had so enthusiastically heralded the appointment of McClellan as general-in-chief, did not mention that Halleck had replaced McClellan.

Burnside's replacement, Hooker, had bargained with Lincoln to receive no orders through Halleck, whom he detested. Before appointing Hooker, Lincoln had not consulted Halleck. Hooker's removal after Chancellorsville was foreshadowed by the reinstitution of Halleck's authority. Again with Meade, Halleck served as a conduit to convey Lincoln's disgust with the failure of the Army of the Potomac to pursue and crush Lee after the battle of Gettysburg. Like every previous commander of the Army of the Potomac, Meade came to detest Halleck.

In the West, Halleck had a slightly different dimension. His strong sense of professionalism assisted Grant during his Vicksburg campaign. Grant faced pressure from two directions. Lincoln believed that his former congressman, General John McClernand, deserved an opportunity to command an expedition against Vicksburg. McClernand had negotiated with Lincoln to command troops recruited from among his Democratic followers in the Midwest. Halleck did everything possible to frustrate McClernand's dream of an independent command. Removed from command on a technicality in June, McClernand appealed in vain to Halleck.

When Grant finally maneuvered his command to high ground south of Vicksburg, Lincoln wanted Grant to unite his

---

[25] Lincoln to Halleck, 1 January 1863, Basler, ed., *Collected Works*, 6:31.

Ulysses S. Grant
(Courtesy of *The Abraham Lincoln Museum*)

command with that of General Nathaniel Banks, then besieging Port Hudson in Louisiana. Halleck's belief that operations were best left to generals in the field worked in Grant's favor, as did his dislike for all political generals. When Vicksburg fell, Lincoln wrote to Grant a celebrated letter acknowledging "you were right and I was wrong."[26] By implication, at least, Lincoln acknowledged that Halleck, also, had been right.

In March 1864 Grant replaced Halleck as general-in-chief as he assumed the rank of lieutenant general. Wary of violating the Constitution, Congress had created this rank without specifying who should receive the appointment. Concerned about creating a rival candidate for the Republican nomination for president, Lincoln first required assurances that Grant held no political ambitions. Lincoln had the option of promoting Halleck without altering command relationship, but called him a "first-rate clerk" who had "shrunk from responsibility wherever it was possible."[27] When Grant was appointed, Halleck immediately resigned as general-in-chief, but Grant, who professed "great confidence in and friendship for" Halleck, cooperated with Lincoln to have Halleck appointed chief of staff.[28] Since Grant intended to stay away from Washington, Halleck's appointment freed Grant from office chores, frequent communication with Lincoln and Stanton, and potential political pressure. Grant had Halleck's assistance in purging such political generals such as Banks, Franz Sigel and Benjamin F. Butler.

Halleck's achievements as a military manager vanished in July when Lee sent Jubal Early to threaten Washington. Halleck dithered while Early moved ever closer. When an anxious Lincoln conferred with Grant at Fort Monroe, Halleck was left behind. As a result, Grant sent General Philip Sheridan to take

[26] Lincoln to Grant, 13 July 1863, ibid., 326.
[27] 24 March, 28 April 1864, *Lincoln and the Civil War in the Diaries and Letters of John Hay*, Tyler Dennett, ed. (New York: Dodd, Mead, 1939) 167, 176.
[28] John A. Rawlins to Elihu B. Washburne, 20 January 1864, James Harrison Wilson, *The Life of John A. Rawlins* (New York: Neale, 1916) 387.

command of all forces near Washington to pursue Early "to the death."[29] Shortly afterward, Grant recommended that Halleck take command on the Pacific Coast.[30]

Grant and Lincoln drew closer while Halleck sat at his desk amid diminished expectations of his role. When Lee surrendered and Grant returned to Washington, Halleck's role disappeared. Following Lincoln's assassination, Stanton immediately sent Halleck to command at Richmond, as if to exile him from the capital. While there, Halleck quarreled with Sherman, his last and most loyal friend among senior commanders.

In less than three years, Halleck's reputation changed from potential savior of the Union to pariah. Shortly after arriving in Washington, Halleck demonstrated an incapacity to direct McClellan or, indeed, any major commander. Why did Halleck remain in Washington? Offered an opportunity by Grant to take command from Banks, Halleck avoided the assignment, perhaps aware that whatever his failings as a desk general, he performed even worse in the field.

Why, then, did Lincoln retain his services? Halleck remained a master of military technique, adept at moving troops and supplies. He knew how to translate Lincoln's directions into proper orders and to offer suggestions about minor matters. He provided Lincoln with a buffer against senior commanders; Halleck's name consistently appeared upon orders for removal. Halleck persistently opposed uniformed politicians, whereas Lincoln unified wartime support by appointing officers for political or ethnic reasons. Halleck received blame when they fell, again protecting Lincoln. As chief of staff, Halleck performed a similar task for Grant, offering counsel concerning the removal of political appointees, warning Grant against moving too quickly or with imprudent timing. Critics who assailed Halleck's weakness and ineptitude rarely noticed that he shielded Lincoln, who once proclaimed himself "Halleck's friend because nobody else was."[31]

---

[29] Grant to Halleck, 1 August 1864, *Papers*, ed. Simon, 11: 358.
[30] Grant to Edwin M. Stanton, 15 August 1864, ibid., 422.
[31] Noah Brooks, *Washington in Lincoln's Time* (org. 1895; New York: Rinehart & Co., 1958) 43.

The otherwise friendless Halleck had not sought the post of general-in-chief. He admitted that he did not "understand and cannot manage affairs in the East," especially "the quarrels of Stanton and McClellan."[32] Lincoln summoned Halleck to Washington to force McClellan to advance or to remove him from command; Halleck's hesitation to choose between these alternatives transferred the initiative to Lee for his great victory at Second Bull Run. Halleck then appealed to McClellan "to assist me in this crisis with your ability and experience. I am utterly tired out."[33] Lincoln later said that Halleck "broke down" after Pope's defeat, "and has ever since evaded all possible responsibility."[34]

Many found Halleck's personal manner obnoxious; few thought that he might have some serious problem. Attorney General Edward Bates heard gossip in 1863 that Halleck "was a confirmed *opium-eater*." Bates noted that Halleck was "something bloated, and with watery eyes,...But whether from brandy or opium I cannot tell."[35] Halleck's personal physician during the Corinth campaign recalled him as "somewhat inert; he was fond of good living, and of good wine—notably of hock. After dining, he was often sleepy. From my own knowledge of him, I think that at first I overestimated him."[36] During Early's campaign against Washington, Charles A. Dana believed that "Halleck's mind has been seriously impaired by the excessive use of liquor and that as a general thing it is regularly muddled after dinner each day."[37] George Templeton Strong had accompanied a delegation to Washington that called on Halleck. "God help us!" exclaimed one member after leaving, something the entire group understood. Halleck was "weak, shallow, commonplace, vulgar," concluded Strong. "His silly talk was conclusive as to his incapacity, unless he was a little flustered

[32] Halleck to William T. Sherman, 16 July 1862, *Official Records*, Ser. I, vol. 17, pt. 2, 100.
[33] Halleck to McClellan, 31 August 1862, ibid., I, 11, pt. 1, 103.
[34] 28 April 1864, Hay, *Diary*, 176.
[35] Howard K. Beale, ed., *The Diary of Edward Bates* (Washington, DC: US Government Printing Office, 1933) 293.
[36] *Personal Memoirs of John H. Brinton* (New York: Neale, 1914) 166.
[37] Dana to John A. Rawlins, 12 July 1864, *Papers*, Simon, ed., 11:231.

with wine ..."[38] Halleck died in 1872 just short of his fifty-seventh birthday "of softening of the Brain supervening upon chronic disease of the *heart* and of the *liver.*"[39]

Halleck's curiously passive behavior in the decade following Pope's defeat supports a theory that he may have had problems with alcohol. When Grant assumed the position of general-in-chief, Halleck quietly accepted the diminished role of chief of staff, and he uttered no protest when sent from Washington to Richmond or into postwar exile in California. When other commanders roundly condemned his wartime role, Halleck made no response. The general who so carefully avoided combat even more assiduously shunned the battle of ideas. Ironically, Halleck's incapacity to operate independently increased his value to Lincoln, who always dominated war policy even when he needed to conceal his mastery.

[38] 24 September 1862, *Diary of George Templeton Strong*, Alan Nevins and Milton Halsey Thomas, eds. (New York: MacMillan, 1952) 3:258.
[39] Jack D. Welsh, *Medical Histories of Union Generals* (Kent OH: Kent State University Press, 1996) 146.

4

LINCOLN AND RACE RELATIONS

By Hans L. Trefousse

In recent years, the problem of race relations in the United States has become steadily more important. Not that it was not crucial before, but in an ever more competitive world, in which the United States has achieved a leading position, the essential flaw in America's vaunted democracy—the persistence of racial prejudice and its resulting difficulties—is now even more significant than previously. In view of this fact, the failure of post-Civil War Reconstruction, America's first attempt at racial justice, would seem to be more ominous than ever, and this failure might have been prevented had President Abraham Lincoln not been assassinated at the very hour of Northern victory.

John Wilkes Booth, it now appears, shot much better than he knew. Having long plotted to kidnap the president, he made up his mind to go ahead with his alternate plan of assassination when he was present at the White House when Lincoln delivered his last speech. Hearing the president advocate limited black suffrage for Louisiana, he asked Lewis Payne, one of his henchmen who was with him, to shoot the speaker right away. Failing to get the wanted reaction, he turned to his other companion, David Herold, and said, "That means nigger citizenship. Now, by God, I'll put him through." Vowing that it would be the last speech Lincoln ever made, three days later the actor killed the president at Ford's Theater.[1]

---

[1] William Hanchett, *The Lincoln Murder Conspiracies* (Urbana and Chicago: 1983) 37.

The immediate consequence of the crime was the accession of Andrew Johnson, the only Senator from a seceding state to remain loyal to the Union. Born a poor white in North Carolina, Johnson was apprenticed to a tailor at the age of ten, ran away from his master a few years later, and eventually migrated to Eastern Tennessee, where he married, set up his own tailor shop, and ultimately acquired wealth and prominence. Elected repeatedly to the state legislature and to Congress as a Democrat, he became governor in 1853, was reelected in 1855, and in 1857 sent to the United States Senate. Reflecting the sentiments of his East Tennessee neighbors who voted against secession, he refused to go with his state in 1861 and became a hero in the North. In 1862 Lincoln appointed him military governor of Tennessee, and in 1864 he won the vice presidency as Lincoln's running mate.[2]

Johnson   His loyalty, however, did not mean that he failed to share his constituents' pronounced racism. He had been a slaveholder himself and was convinced that the blacks were inherently inferior to the whites, a prejudice he had made abundantly clear in 1844 in the House of Representatives, when he said, "If one portion of the community were to be masters another menials…., he had no hesitancy in bringing his mind to a conclusion on the subject, believing, as he did, that the black race of Africa were inferior to the white man in point of intellect-better calculated in physical structure to undergo drudgery and hardship–standing as they do, many degrees lower in the scale of gradation that expresses the relative relation between God and all that He has created than the white man." If the laws did not distinguish between white and black, they would "place every spay-footed, bandy-shanked, hump-backed, thick-lipped, flat-nosed, woolly headed, ebon-colored negro in the country upon an equality with the poor white man."[3] And although during the 1864 campaign he told the blacks he might be their Moses to lead them out of bondage,[4] he never abandoned his prejudices and as late as 1868 still complained to his private

[2] Hans L. Trefousse, *Andrew Johnson: A Biography* (New York: 1989).
[3] *Congressional Globe*, 28th Congress, 1st Sess., App. 95-98.
[4] Leroy P. Graf, ed., *The Papers of Andrew Johnson* (Knoxville: The University of Tennessee Press, 1967 –) 7:251-53.

secretary, Colonel W. G. Moore, that blacks and not whites were employed on the grounds of the White House. He was determined to keep the South a white man's country, and it might well be argued that he fully achieved that aim.[5]

Now it so happened, as Professor Thomas Turner has so well shown, that the period following the assassination was one not only of deep mourning but also of greatly aggravated feelings toward the defeated South, held responsible for the atrocious deed.[6] Not knowing what was in store for them, Southerners, stunned by events, were ready to accept almost any conditions, including even black suffrage, to restore peace and quiet.[7] Had Lincoln been alive, he might well have used this feeling to set a new course for the defeated section, and there is little doubt that it would have been different from Johnson's plan of Reconstruction, or rather, restoration, as he preferred to call it, which was so mild that Southerners immediately began to oppose concessions to the freedmen, particularly the franchise.

The reasons for assuming this pronounced difference between the two executives are clear. Lincoln's attitude toward the race question was the exact opposite of that of his successor. In the first place, unlike Johnson, who had been a defender of slavery until war time necessities caused him to espouse emancipation, Lincoln had always abhorred slavery. As early as 1837, he was one of two members of the Illinois legislature to condemn the "peculiar institution" as "founded on injustice and bad policy."[8] In 1849, he prepared a bill for the emancipation of the slaves in the District of Columbia, and in 1854 in his famous Peoria Address he again denounced the institution in no uncertain terms.[9] His subsequent campaigns and speeches in Illinois and elsewhere rarely omitted a castigation of bondage, culminating in his antislavery campaign against Stephen A.

---

[5] 9 April 1868, W. G. Moore, Diary, Johnson Papers, LC.

[6] Thomas R. Turner, *Beware of the People Weeping: Public Opinion and the Assassination of Abraham Lincoln* (Baton Rouge: Louisiana State University Press: 1982).

[7] C. Van Woodward, ed., *Whitelaw Reid, After the War: A Tour of the Southern States, 1865-1866* (New York: 1965) 44.

[8] Roy P. Basler, ed., *The Collected Works of Abraham Lincoln* (New Brunswick: 1953) 1:74-75.

[9] Ibid., 2:20-22.

Douglas in 1858. Finally in 1860 he was elected president on a platform pledging an end to the extension of slavery.

It is true that Lincoln never, prior to 1862, advocated federal action to end slavery in the states where it existed. Constitutional obligations were important to him, and he hoped that putting an end to the expansion of the institution would in the end cause its demise in the South. As he said in his famous House Divided Against Itself Speech at Springfield in June 1858, "I believe this government cannot endure, permanently half slave and half free. I do not expect the Union to be dissolved; I do not expect the house to fall, but I do expect it will cease to be divided. It will become all one thing or all the other. Either the opponents of slavery will arrest the further spread of it, and place it where the public mind shall rest in the belief that it is in course of ultimate extinction, or its advocates will push it forward, till it shall become alike lawful in all the States, old as well as new–North as well as South." He then deplored the apparent tendency to the "latter condition," and in the winter of 1860 refused to entertain any compromise involving the further spread of slavery.[10]

While president, Lincoln, for reasons of political necessity, emphasized that the war was fought, not for the abolition of slavery, but for the preservation of the Union, he never wavered from his conviction that slavery was wrong. In view of the fact that he had been elected by a minority of some thirty-nine percent of the voters, most of whom had no sympathy with abolitionism, and that he had to retain their loyalty, he could not emphasize his antislavery convictions. This was especially true because he was anxious to retain the border slave states–he is reputed to have said that he hoped God was on his side but he must have Kentucky–and any antislavery move would have heightened the danger of further secessions.[11] Nevertheless, there were various instances in which he could still show that he had hardly abandoned his long held views, and he rarely hesitated to do so. Even though he had stated in his first

---

[10] Ibid., 2:461-69.
[11] James McPherson, *Battle Cry of Freedom: The Civil War Era* (New York: Oxford University Press, 1988) 284.

inaugural that he had no intention of interfering with slavery in the states where it existed, in his first address to Congress on 4 July 1861, while repeating this purpose, he added that after the suppression of the rebellion he "probably" would have no different understanding of his powers.[12] Little more than a month later, he signed the first Confiscation Bill freeing bondsmen used by the Confederates against the United States;[13] then, in December 1861 he asked the lone representative from Delaware to inaugurate a scheme of compensated emancipation in that border state, and in March 1862 made this suggestion publicly to apply to all the border states.[14] And while none of these saw fit to accept his suggestion, in April he signed a bill freeing the slaves in the District of Columbia, followed in June by one abolishing the institution in the territories. And although he hesitated to sign the second Confiscation Act, freeing the slaves of all insurgents, after insisting on certain modifications, he approved of it also.[15]

It is true that during this entire period Lincoln did not hesitate to revoke orders of individual generals seeking to effect emancipation on their own. In September 1861 he annulled John C. Fremont's edict for this purpose in Missouri, and in May 1862 a similar order by David Hunter in the Department of the South.[16] These steps, however, were merely taken for political reasons, and by June 1862 he had decided that the time was ripe to go further. Preparing his Emancipation Proclamation freeing slaves in areas still in rebellion within a given time, he submitted it to the cabinet in July. Advised to postpone it until the federal army had achieved some victory, he issued it on 22 September in his capacity as commander-in-chief of the army and navy to go into effect within one hundred days.[17] If shortly before the publication of the Preliminary Proclamation he still gave his well known reply to Horace Greeley's "The

[12] Basler, ed., *Collected Works*, 2:263, 439.
[13] James McPherson, *The Political History of the United States During the Great Rebellion, 1860-1865* (Washington: 1865) 195-96.
[14] Basler, ed., *Collected Works*, 5:28-31, 144-46.
[15] *Great Rebellion*, McPherson, 212-13, 254-55, 196-98.
[16] Ibid., 245-47, 251.
[17] Hans L. Trefousse, *Lincoln's Decision for Emancipation* (Philadelphia: 1975) 35-38, 44-46, 89-91.

Prayer of Twenty Millions" in which he stated that his primary purpose was to save the Union, and that he would do so if it meant freeing all slaves, some of the slaves, or none of the slaves, he nevertheless added that he had merely given his opinion of public duty and that he intended no edification of his "oft-expressed personal wish that all men everywhere could be free."[18]

The final proclamation followed on 1 January 1863, and having already told a delegation of Kentuckians that he would rather die than to take back a word of it, he made it known that he would never repeal it. He affirmed its validity to James C. Conkling in August 1863, and in April of the next year wrote to A. G. Hodges, "If slavery is not wrong, nothing is wrong."[19] He exerted pressure on the governors of the states exempt from the proclamation to take steps to abolish the institution in their own jurisdictions, while making the acceptance of the proclamation a condition for his offer of amnesty to insurgents.[20] In 1864 he assented to his renomination on a platform endorsing a constitutional amendment for the abolition of slavery, signed the bill repealing the Fugitive Slave Law, and after his reelection, he used the full powers of his office to secure the adoption of the amendment in the House of Representatives which had failed to secure the necessary two-thirds vote in the previous session. Thus there is little doubt about his detestation of the "peculiar institution"[21]

Lincoln's views on race are less unequivocal. Born in a slave state and raised in deeply racist southern Indiana, he could hardly have escaped the all-present notions of racial inequality which in the nineteenth century prevailed not only in the United States but throughout the world. Considering the fact that modern anthropological findings about the equality of human races did not appear until after the turn of the century, it is

---

18 Basler, ed., *Collected Works*, 5:388-89.
19 Ibid., 5:503; 6:28-31, 281, 406-10.
20 Trefousse, *Lincoln's Decision for Emancipation*, 53-54; Basler, ed., *Collected Works*, 7:53-56.
21 J. G. Randall and Richard N. Current, *Lincoln the President: Last Full Measure* (New York: 1955) 302 ff.; McPherson, *Great Rebellion*, 237, 406.

not surprising that hardly anybody espoused them previously. To be sure, there were a few abolitionists and foes of slavery who preached the doctrine of human equality–Charles Sumner, Wendell Phillips, Thaddeus Stevens, and Gerrit Smith, for example–but they were an exception and even many opponents of human bondage were not free from prejudice.[22] Consequently, Lincoln too was affected by his surroundings and prior to the Civil War never advocated full racial equality.

But in spite of this failure, he never made a point of racism, as so many of his opponents were wont to do.[23] Whether equal to the whites or not, he always considered the African-Americans human beings, and not a separate species. In 1841 while returning from a trip to Kentucky, he observed some slaves who were being taken down the river. As he described the incident to the sister of his friend Joshua Speed, a fine example was presented on board the boat for contemplating the effect of *condition* upon human happiness. A gentleman had purchased twelve Negroes in different parts of Kentucky and was taking them to a farm in the South. They were chained six and six together. A small iron clevis was around the left wrist of each, and this fastened to the main chain by a shorter one at a convenient distance from, the others; so that the Negroes were strung together precisely like so many fish on a trot-line. In this condition they were being separated forever from the scenes of their childhood, their friends, their fathers and mothers, and brothers and sisters, and many of them, from their wives and children, and going into perpetual slavery where the lash of the master is proverbially more ruthless and unrelenting than any other where; and yet amid all these distressing circumstances, as we would think of them, they were the most cheerful and apparently happy creatures on board. One, whose offense for which he had been sold was an over-fondness for his wife,

---

[22] Hans L. Trefousse, *The Radical Republicans: Lincoln's Vanguard for Racial Justice* (New York: 1969) 28-33; James Brewer Stewart, *Holy Warriors: The Abolitionists and American Slavery* (New York: 1976) 105; Oscar Sherwin, *Prophet of Liberty: The Life and Time of Wendell Phillips* (New York: 1958) 272; Fawn Brodie, *Thaddeus Stevens, Scourge of the South* (New York: 1959) 109.
[23] Cf. LaWanda Cox, *Lincoln and Black Freedom: A Study in Presidential Leadership* (Columbia SC: 1981) 20 ff.

played the fiddle almost continually; and the others danced, sang, cracked jokes, and played various games with cards from day to day: "How true it is that 'God tempers the wind to the shorn lamb', or in other words, that He renders the worst of human conditions tolerable, while He permits the best, to be nothing better than tolerable."

Even though in later years, he recalled the incident as an affront to him because of its cruelty, at the time he was more interested in its illustration of human psychology and obviously considered the subject of race a fit example for such observations.[24]

His unusually liberal racial views can again be illustrated by a fragment on slavery which he probably wrote in 1854. Asking if "A" could prove that by right he might enslave "B," why then was not the same thing true the other way around? If the answer were color, then the first man with a skin fairer than "A's" might be justified in enslaving him. If the answer were not color, but the assumption that whites were intellectually superior to the blacks, then "A" would be a slave to the first person he met with an intellect superior to his. Lincoln's racial feelings were obviously very malleable.[25]

In 1855 he again gave an example of his tolerance. He said he was not a Know Nothing, for how could anyone who abhorred the oppression of Negroes be in favor of degrading classes of white people. "As a nation," he continued, "we began by declaring that 'all men are created equal.' We now practically read it 'all men are created equal, except negroes.' When the Know Nothings get control, it will read 'all men are created equal, except negroes, and foreigners, and Catholics.' When it comes to this, I should prefer emigrating to some country where they make no pretence of loving liberty–to Russia, for instance, where despotism can be taken pure, and without the base alloy of hypocrisy."

The future Great Emancipator again clarified his notions of equality by stating in 1857 that because he did not want a black

---

[24] Basler, ed., *Collected Works*, 1:259-61; Richard N. Current, *The Lincoln Nobody Knows* (New York: 1958) 218.
[25] Basler, ed., *Collected Works*, 1:222-23.

woman for a slave he must necessarily want her for a wife. "I need not have her for either," he continued. "I can just leave her alone. In some respects she is certainly not my equal; but in her natural right to eat the bread she earns with her own hands without asking leave of anyone else, she is my equal and equal of all others." He repeated this sentiment several times, unusual though it was for the age. In addition, in 1858 he pleaded, "let us discard all this quibbling...about this race and the other race being inferior, and therefore must be placed in an inferior position–discarding our standard that we have left us. Let us discard all these things, and unite as one people throughout this land, until we shall once more stand up declaring that all men are created equal."[26]

Advanced as these sentiments were, not even Lincoln could, in a political campaign, advocate the social equality of the blacks. This political reality was especially true during his debates with Senator Douglas, when, at Charleston, answering questions about his views, he replied, "I will say then, that I am not, nor ever have been in favor of bringing about the equality of the white and black races–that I am not nor ever have been in favor of making voters or jurors of negroes, nor of qualifying them to hold office, nor to intermarry with white people; and I will say in addition to this that there is a physical difference between the white and black races which I believe will forever forbid the two races living together on terms of social and political equality. And inasmuch as they cannot so live, while they do remain together there must be the position of superior and inferior, and I as much as every other man am in favor of having the superior position assigned to the white race." These remarks have often been quoted to prove that Lincoln was a thorough racist, but they must be compared with Douglas' incessant harping on black inferiority, his insistence that a Negro could never be a citizen because of belonging to a race incapable of self government. As he said to make his point clear, "Why, they brought Fred Douglass to Freeport when I was addressing a meeting there in a carriage driven by the white owner, the negro sitting inside with the white lady and

[26] Ibid., 2:322-33, 405, 498; 3:146; 2:501.

her daughter." His remarks had the desired effect. They elicited cries of "Shame" from the racist audience.[27]

During the 1860 presidential campaign and its secession aftermath, the race question was somewhat muted, but after the outbreak of Civil War, it could not long be disregarded. The question of what to do with the blacks who entered Union lines, or, following the Emancipation Proclamation, who were freed, had to be met. As early as August 1862 Lincoln sought to meet this problem by suggesting colonization of blacks outside of the United States, a solution which had long been advocated by Whigs such as Henry Clay, whom he admired. Whether the president really believed in the feasibility of this course of action or whether he utilized it to assuage the conservatives is not quite clear, but he did invite a number of black leaders to the White House to ask them to initiate the process. The very fact that he invited blacks to the executive mansion showed his lack of pronounced racial prejudice, and the way he presented the problem to his guests reinforced this point. "You and we are different races," he told them. "We have between us a broader difference than exists between almost any other two races. Whether it is right or wrong, I need not discuss, but this physical difference is a great disadvantage to us both, as I think your race suffer very greatly, many of them by living among us, while ours suffers from your presence." He then continued by deploring the wrong inflicted upon the blacks and pointing out that even when free they were not treated as equals. Thus separation might be the answer.[28] Nothing came of this particular interview, but some time later, Lincoln did initiate the colonization of Ile la Vache off Haiti, an experiment that ended in utter failure and his sending vessels to bring back the survivors.[29]

In 1863 he had the opportunity of meeting the famous black abolitionist Frederick Douglass, who had come to the White House to seek better treatment for black troops. Not knowing

---

[27] Ibid., 3:145-46; 3:105 (Douglas' remarks); Don E. Fehrenbacher, "Only His Stepchildren: Lincoln and the Negro," *Civil War History*, 20 (1974): 298.

[28] Basler, ed., *Collected Works*, 5:370-75.

[29] Benjamin P. Thomas, *Abraham Lincoln* (New York: 1952) 363.

how he would be received, he was uneasy, but Lincoln quickly put him at ease. Arising from his chair, he offered Douglass his hand and bade him welcome. He then listened to his visitor's complaints and promised to do what he could. Douglass was deeply impressed and even more so when on another occasion Lincoln, discussing matters with the black leader, made Governor William A. Buckingham of Connecticut wait in spite of Douglass' pleading that he should see the other visitor first. Whatever racial prejudices Lincoln may have had were rapidly becoming less pronounced than ever, as he showed during his second inaugural when Douglass, attempting to be admitted to the evening's festivities, was rudely rejected by the guards on duty. Lincoln, on being informed of the African-American's presence, interfered and said, "Here comes my friend Douglass. I am glad to see you." Ushering him in, he asked him what Douglass thought of the inaugural address, telling him there was no man in the country whose opinion he valued more. As Douglass wrote, "In his company, I was never reminded of my humble origin, or of my unpopular color.[30]

There were other indications that Lincoln's ideas on race were rapidly becoming more flexible than ever. One of the most radical propositions in 1864 was the proposal to enfranchise the freedmen. In spite of his political caution, the president gradually came to the conclusion that he ought to further the idea. As he wrote to James Wadsworth, probably in January, "I cannot see, if universal amnesty is granted, how, under the circumstances, I can avoid exacting in return universal suffrage, or at least, suffrage on the basis of intelligence and military service." And in March of the same year, he admonished Governor Michael Hahn of the new Free State Government of Louisiana to see if the suffrage could not be extended to the more intelligent blacks and to those who fought for the Union. At the time, it was still too early to make his views public, but in his last speech, he recurred to them and

[30] Frederick Douglass, *Autobiographies* (New York: 1994) 785, 797, 802 ff.

publicly announced his convictions about the desirability of suffrage for some of the freedmen.[31]

It is of course impossible to know what would have happened had Lincoln lived. In a brilliant chapter in her book, *Lincoln and Black Freedom*, LaWanda Cox has tried to speculate about this problem and came to the conclusion that not even the president might have been successful.[32] Yet, it is equally clear that, despite many assertions to the contrary, he would not have committed Johnson's faults. As Carl Schurz summed it up so well,

> Had he [Lincoln] lived, he would have as ardently wished to stop bloodshed and to reunite all the states, as he ever did. But is it to be supposed for a moment that, seeing the late master class in the South, still under the influence of their old traditional notions and prejudices and at the same time sorely pressed by the distressing necessities of their situation, intent upon subjecting the freedmen again to a system very much akin to slavery, Lincoln would have consented to abandon these freedmen to the mercies of that master class? Can it be imagined that he would have been deaf to the sinister reports coming up from the South, as Johnson was? Would he have sacrificed the rights of the emancipated slaves and the security of the Union men to a metaphysical abstraction as to the indestructibility of states? Did he not repeatedly warn against the mere discussion of just such abstractions as something useless and misleading? To assert in the face of all this that the Johnson Reconstruction policy was only Lincoln's policy continued, is little less than a perversion of historic truth.[33]

Thus Lincoln's death was indeed a disaster. It removed the one statesman who, because of his political genius, might have

[31] Basler, ed., *Collected Works*, 7:101, 243.
[32] Cox, *Lincoln and Black Freedom*, 142-84.
[33] Frederick Bancroft and William A. Dunning, *The Reminiscences of Carl Schurz* (New York: 1908) 3:222-23.

succeeded in effecting some sort of solution of the problem posed by some four million freedmen. His successor was not primarily interested in this question, and the result was a calamity for the United States, for race relations, and the integration of the freedmen into American society.

5

"SOMETHING MORE THAN THE MERE 'UNION' TO FIGHT FOR:" AFRICAN AMERICANS RESPOND TO LINCOLN'S WARTIME POLICIES

by Edna Greene Medford

> I have no purpose, directly or indirectly, to interfere with the institution of slavery in the States where it exists. I believe I have no lawful right to do so, and I have no inclination to do so.[1]

Quoting from one of his 1858 senatorial debates with fellow Illinoisan Stephen A. Douglas, Abraham Lincoln used the occasion of his first inaugural address to assure the recently seceded Southern states (and those contemplating secession) that he intended no hostile action against their system of unfree labor. His assertions failed to placate Southerners fearful of this new administration elected on an antislavery platform. Neither did his hands-off policy reassure those abolitionists who saw in the South's attempt to dissolve the Union far-reaching implications for the nearly four million enslaved African Americans who lived and labored in the newly-formed Confederacy and the

---

[1] Quoted from Lincoln's First Inaugural Address, in Roy Basler, ed., *The Collected Works of Abraham Lincoln* (New Brunswick: Rutgers University Press, 1953) 4:250. Lincoln had initially made the remark in Ottawa, Illinois on 21 August 1858, as the first in a series of debates with the incumbent senator Stephen A. Douglas.

Stephen A. Douglas
(Courtesy of *The Abraham Lincoln Museum*)

border states. While many Americans viewed the developing split between North and South with trepidation, those who hoped the conflict inevitably would lead to the death of slavery welcomed war as an opportunity for "all the righteous forces of the nation to deal a death-blow to the monster evil of the nineteenth century."[2] Once war commenced, the proponents of black freedom pressed Lincoln to abandon his insistence on keeping the struggle one simply to preserve the Union.[3]

Although the political power and racial acceptability of white abolitionists eventually enabled them to shape public opinion and effectively press Lincoln to alter his prosecution of the war, Northern blacks' responses to the president's policies exhibited a poignancy born of the African American's unique and personal stake in the outcome of the conflict. For them, advocacy of freedom for enslaved people was more than an intellectual exercise or defense of lofty principles long abandoned by the rest of the nation. Many Northern blacks (especially the leaders) had themselves suffered under slavery's grip, left relatives behind as they made their escape to the North, and had managed through sheer determination to elevate themselves. Yet, they lacked the full citizenship rights guaranteed to other free men. Their insistence on making freedom and equality the central focus of the war reflected a concern both for the enslaved masses in the South as well as the potential for elevation of their own status. Hence, despite their numerical disadvantage and their inaccessibility to the seat of power, Northern blacks became vociferous critics of presidential policies they felt hindered their ultimate goal.

The African American campaign for freedom and liberty drew upon the talents of a group of men which included both the free born and those who had spent their formative years in bondage. Frederick Douglass, the most renowned among them,

---

[2] Frederick Douglass, "The Fall of Sumter," in Philip S. Foner, ed., *The Life and Writings of Frederick Douglass: The Civil War, 1861-1865* (New York: International Publishers, 1975) 3:91.

[3] For discussion primarily of the role of white abolitionists during the war, see James M. McPherson, *The Struggle for Equality: Abolitionists and the Negro in the Civil War and Reconstruction* (Princeton: Princeton University Press, 1964).

had spent his childhood and adolescent years alternately in the rural environs of Maryland's Eastern Shore and in the antebellum South's most populous city–Baltimore.[4] Learning to read and write, despite laws forbidding the educating of enslaved people, he vowed to seek freedom at the earliest opportunity. At the age of twenty, his moment came; Douglass escaped to New York.[5] Eventually he joined the antislavery lecture circuit and traveled widely, giving his personal account of life in bondage. By mid-century, he had tried his hand at editing and publishing an antislavery newspaper. Throughout the war, he used the appropriately titled *Douglass' Monthly* to level indictments against Lincoln and his policies.

Other formerly enslaved black abolitionists included James W.C. Pennington, who in 1854 had unsuccessfully challenged the discriminatory transportation system in New York; Henry Highland Garnet, pastor of New York's Shiloh Presbyterian Church; Jermain W. Loguen of the African Methodist Episcopal Church in Syracuse, and H. Ford Douglas, a 28 year old antislavery lecturer who resided in Illinois. In 1843, while attending the Negro National Convention, Garnet had stunned more conservative abolitionists when he advocated an enslaved person's right to resist his bondage and hinted at the possibility of violent overthrow of the system.[6] Less radical, perhaps, but equally dedicated to the cause of black liberation, Loguen had defied the 1850 Fugitive Slave law by assisting runaways. As manager of the Fugitive Aid Society of Syracuse, he had sought jobs for those attempting to start lives as free men and women in the North.[7] Despite his youth, H. Ford Douglas had already earned a reputation as an effective lecturer. His fiery rhetoric matched (and occasionally eclipsed) the anti-slavery oratory of his elders.

---

[4] By 1860, Baltimore was also home to the largest number of free blacks in the nation.

[5] Douglass' early life is treated by Dickson J. Preston in *Young Frederick Douglass: The Maryland Years* (Baltimore: Johns Hopkins University Press, 1980).

[6] See Joel Schor, *Henry Highland Garnet: A Voice of Black Radicalism in the Nineteenth Century* (Westport CT: Greenwood Press, 1977) 53-60.

[7] Benjamin Quarles, *Black Abolitionists* (New York: Oxford University Press, 1969) 154.

Among the free-born black abolitionists was Thomas Hamilton, editor of the New York-based *Weekly Anglo-African*, whose motto was, "Man Must Be Free–If Not Through Law, Why Then Above The Law"; James McCune Smith, a prominent New York doctor and author who had been trained in Europe; and George T. Downing, son of the wealthy New York restaurateur Thomas Downing, and a successful caterer himself.[8] Although less intimately associated with slavery, these men shared with the former bondsmen-turned-abolitionists a commitment to destroy the institution and end the discrimination that characterized their own "free" lives.

The man whom African Americans hoped would become a champion of freedom and liberty was no abolitionist. Although he ran on an anti-slavery platform in the 1860 presidential campaign, Lincoln's position on slavery was a moderate one. While opposing its extension, he believed that he had no constitutional right to interfere with it where it already existed.[9] His position on slavery forced black voters to face a difficult question in the 1860 election: Could they cast a vote for the Republican candidate because of the party's anti-slavery sentiment without endorsing those aspects of its platform that could be construed as pro-slavery? The issue was debated in the columns of black newspapers, from pulpits, and from the speakers' platforms at anti-slavery meetings. The following letter sent to the *Weekly Anglo-African* hints at the dilemma people of color faced:

> [W]hile there is much to excite our interest, not to say anxiety, there is nothing to elicit our sympathies towards either of the contending hosts. By these we are

[8] James McPherson (*The Negro's Civil War: How American Negroes Felt and Acted during the War for the Union* [Urbana: University of Illinois Press, 1982]) provides a glimpse of the attitudes and activities of some of these men through documentary excerpts. See also Benjamin Quarles, *Lincoln and the Negro* (New York: Oxford University Press, 1962).

[9] See Letter from Lincoln to Joshua F. Speed, Springfield, 24 August 1855, reprinted in Richard N. Current, ed., *The Political Thought of Abraham Lincoln* (Indianapolis: Bobbs-Merrill Company, 1967) 79-83; see also Lincoln's First Inaugural Address, reprinted in Basler, ed., *Collected Works*, 250.

disliked as slaves, by those disliked as freemen.... We are reduced to the necessity of choosing between two evils, and as every vote withheld from the Republican side is virtually thrown in favor of the Democracy, I think we ought...to cooperate in their [Republicans'] efforts to cripple the power we would fain destroy–not that we dislike prejudice less, but that we hate slavery more.[10]

Frederick Douglass echoed this sentiment when he advised readers of *Douglass' Monthly* to work with the Republicans on matters agreeable to all while reserving the right to "do more radical work in the future."[11]

African-Americans expressed interest in the 1860 campaign in disproportion to the size of the black electorate. Black voting strength was kept ineffective, in part, because free people of color comprised so small a portion of the population and because most of the states had taken steps to disenfranchise blacks during the antebellum period. Only in five Northern states – Massachusetts, Maine, New Hampshire, Rhode Island and Vermont – did African-Americans enjoy equal access to the ballot.[12] But realizing that the broader political issues affecting the nation could adversely affect the hopes of blacks, African-Americans followed the campaign closely.[13] Ultimately, some people of color could not bring themselves to vote either for Lincoln or any of the three other principal candidates. H. Ford Douglas, for instance, felt too many negatives argued against his embracing the candidacy of his fellow Illinoisan, but he could not generate any enthusiasm for the other candidates

---

[10] "How Shall We Vote," *The Weekly Anglo-African* (New York), 27 August 1859.

[11] "What is the Duty of Radical Abolitionists in the Present Campaign?" and "Reply to J.C.H.," in *Douglass' Monthly* (October 1860).

[12] McPherson, *The Negro's Civil War*, 3. For treatment of the status of free blacks in the North after the American Revolution, see Leon Litwack, *North of Slavery: The Negro in the Free States, 1790-1860* (Chicago: University of Chicago Press, 1961).

[13] "How Shall We Vote?," *The Weekly Anglo-African* (New York), 27 August 1859.

either. Ultimately, he felt, all four major parties deserved condemnation for not seeking to "lift the negro out of his fetters."[14]

Given the unattractiveness of the major candidates, a few African Americans felt they had no choice but to stand on principle and support the Radical Abolitionist, Gerritt Smith, whose position on federal intervention to abolish slavery won praise from those who argued that the Constitution did not preclude this avenue to emancipation.[15] After having initially expressed hope in Lincoln's intentions, these men shifted their support to Smith. Their apprehensiveness toward the president intensified once the war commenced.

After Lincoln entered the White House, African Americans attempted to maintain some level of optimism but steeled themselves for disappointment. The secession from the Union of South Carolina and several other states shortly after the election added a new dimension to their anxiety. Blacks saw Lincoln positioned to do one of two things: either acknowledge the centrality of slavery to the conflict and destroy it to preserve the Union, or he would follow a cautious, conciliatory policy toward the seceded states and secure the very institution that threatened the nation. Lincoln's reticence before the inauguration kept blacks (and the rest of the nation) in suspense.

The president's inaugural address did little to reassure African Americans that he would become the champion of their freedom and equality. If anything, he made a number of points that discouraged them from any inclination toward optimism. In addition to expressing his intention to leave slavery alone where it already existed, Lincoln pledged to uphold the Fugitive Slave Law of 1850, which denied enslaved people certain basic rights (such as trial by jury, testimony in one's

---

[14] H. Ford Douglas, "Lincoln, Slavery, and Equal Rights," in Norton Garfinkle, ed., *Lincoln and the Coming of the Civil War* (Boston: D. C. Heath and Company, 1959) 31-34.
[15] McPherson, *The Negro's Civil War*, 8-9.

FREDERICK DOUGLASS
Orator

Frederick Douglass
(Courtesy of *The Abraham Lincoln Museum*)

own defense, and presumption of innocence) and more effectively involved Northerners in the apprehension of runaways.[16] The law had prompted long-established fugitives from slavery residing in the North to relocate to the safety of Canada.[17] To Lincoln's argument that the main dispute dividing the nation was that "one section of the country believes slavery is right, and ought to be extended, while the other believes it is wrong, and ought not to be extended," Thomas Hamilton responded caustically:

It is slavery, President Lincoln—the wrong done to four and a half millions of human beings—that all this fraternal strife and internecine war is due, and not to the question of extending the crime over a few thousand square leagues more of territory. It is the existence not the extension of slavery that is at issue. The latter is but one of the collateral questions, magnified by adroit politicians into importance to divert and distract the nation from the only vital position–shall slavery live at all?[18]

Hamilton warned that African Americans could not find comfort in Lincoln's address. "The Republican party is for the white man," he allowed. "We must rely on ourselves."[19]

Similarly, a frustrated Frederick Douglass declared the inaugural address "a double-tongued document, capable of two constructions, and conceals rather than declares a definite policy."[20] Accusing Lincoln of courting the favor of the slaveholders, Douglass declared that the president "bends the knee to slavery as readily as any of his infamous predecessors He stands upon the same moral level with [the slaveholders], and is in no respect better than they."[21] Douglass did,

---

[16] Basler, ed., *Collected Works*, 4:250. For a discussion of the role of the Fugitive Slave Law in escalating sectional conflict, see Basler, ed., *Collected Works*, 4:250. Lincoln had initially made the remark in Ottawa, Illinois on 21 August 1858, as the first in a series of debates with the incumbent senator. W. Campbell, *The Slave Catchers: The Enforcement of the Fugitive Slave Law, 1850-1860* (Chapel Hill: University of North Carolina Press, 1968).
[17] Quarles, *Lincoln and the Negro*, 48-50, 61.
[18] "President Lincoln's Inaugural," *Weekly Anglo-African* (New York), 16 March 1861.
[19] Ibid.
[20] "The Inaugural Address," *Douglass' Monthly* (April 1861): 434.
[21] Ibid.

however, find reason for a small measure of optimism in
Lincoln's suggestion that safeguards be put in place to ensure
that free men would not be taken up as slaves. But given the
larger issues at stake, he found this one consideration a small
consolation.

The failure of Lincoln's conciliatory overtures and the firing
on Fort Sumter renewed African American hopes that the
nation would not be reunited with slavery intact. With war
declared, they sought to ensure a positive outcome for the
Union and themselves by heeding the call to arms. The Hanni-
bal Guards, a group of black men in Pennsylvania, offered
their services to the state militia. Elsewhere, black men
organized themselves into military units and drilled in antici-
pation of being mustered into military service. The states
spurned their offers, and locals, determined to keep it a "white
man's war," threatened violence against any black man intent
on becoming an active participant. Undeterred by this rebuff,
some African Americans pressed onward, determined to seize
the opportunity to influence the outcome of the war. Those less
inclined to fight offered their meager savings to the Union
cause. In New York, for instance, they pledged to pay for, arm,
and equip three regiments of black men who had been organized in that state.[22] In other areas they could offer little more
than prayers.

While patriotism doubtless played some part in the desire of
African Americans to enter the war, they clearly and eloquently
articulated the more personal reasons for their enthusiasm. At a
Cleveland rally, B. K. Sampson offered the following position
on black participation in the conflict:

> The presumption is that we exercise unfaltering devotion to
> the Union; but our patriotism and our hopes arise not from
> the efforts of McClellan nor the Administration…[I] confess
> myself ambitious of the glory of preserving the union of
> these States, but my highest ambition is to strike a death
> blow to slavery…we would fight for more than country, for
> more than a union of states; we would defend more than

[22] Quarles, *Lincoln and the Negro*, 66-68.

human laws, we would defend those which are divine
...That is a noble soul who would lay his life upon the altar
of his country, but nobler far is he who dies to free his
brother man.[23]

Sampson's remarks hint at the ambivalence some African
Americans felt regarding support of the Union. Resentful of the
denial of certain liberties and feeling the sting of the rejection of
their offer of military service, some Northern blacks vowed to
remain neutral, "ever praying for the success of that party
determined to initiate first the policy of justice and equal
rights."[24] Others promised support to the Union only if the
destruction of slavery was made an aim of the war. William
Wells Brown, a former slave, writer, and popular anti-slavery
lecturer, reminded African Americans that they owed their first
duty to the slave and hence were obliged to use their energies
to facilitate his emancipation. Support of the Union was
foolhardy since the government had not shown an inclination to
overthrow slavery.[25] Still others demanded as a condition for
participation greater emphasis on basic rights for people of
color. Until blacks in the North acquired the same rights as
white men, they declared, "we are in no condition to fight
under the flag which gives us no protection."[26]

As aggrieved as African Americans felt, however, they
recognized that their best chance for freedom and equality
rested with the Union. "Should slavery triumph in the nation's
overthrow... comparative safety in our persons, in the posses-
sions of our property and our educational and religious
advantages, are all lost...," they argued. Given the fragility of

---

[23] "Speech of Mr. B. K. Sampson," quoted in the *Weekly Anglo-African* (New York), 9 November 1861.

[24] *The Weekly Anglo-African*, 28 September 1861.

[25] A review of Brown's remarks was printed in the *Weekly Anglo-African* (New York), 4 May 1861.

[26] "'What are we Colored People Doing? Or Likely to Do?' Letter to the Editor from 'Ivanhoe,'" Troy (New York), 7 October 1861, *The Anglo-African*, 19 October 1861.

the liberty they enjoyed in the North, blacks could not be "indifferent spectators to passing events."[27]

But in the first few months of the war it seemed that Lincoln and the North were interested neither in freedom nor equality for people of color. African Americans became particularly dismayed by Lincoln's failure to formulate a definitive policy regarding runaways. Enslaved people had used the cover of war to make their escape to freedom almost from the very beginning of the conflict. With no definite federal policy in place, Union generals formulated their own. While General Benjamin F. Butler justified his decision to confiscate the runaways seeking protection at Fortress Monroe as contraband-of-war, other commanders returned fugitives to their owners, even when the latter were rebels.[28] The practice prompted Frederick Douglass to inquire if the slaveholder's right in his slave was more sacred than his right to his livestock or his food. Douglass saw no rational reason why the "flour and iron of the non-slaveholding merchant of Richmond [should] be seized and appropriated by the Government, while the slave of the slave-holder...is carefully returned to his master, as a piece of property too sacred to lose its character as property."[29] In August 1861, Congress passed the First Confiscation Act which provided for the appropriation of those slaves who had been of direct assistance to the Confederate military. Although Lincoln signed the measure, he insisted that he was the best person to determine concerns involving the slaves.[30] Incredulously, not until the spring of 1862 did Congress pass legislation prohibiting Union officers from returning fugitives who entered the federal lines.[31]

When sympathetic Union generals attempted to move beyond mere confiscation, they met with firm resistance from Lincoln. Such was the case in September 1861, when General

---

[27] Speech of Mr. B. K. Sampson," *Weekly Anglo-African* (New York), 9 November 1861.
[28] Quarles, *Lincoln and the Negro*, 68-70.
[29] "The Position of the Government Toward Slavery," *Douglass' Monthly* (June 1861).
[30] Quarles, *Lincoln and the Negro*, 69-70.
[31] McPherson, *The Negro's Civil War*, 44.

John C. Fremont attempted emancipation in Missouri. As Commander of the Department of the West, Fremont had declared martial law in the border state and had issued a proclamation freeing the slaves of all slaveholders in rebellion. Lincoln countermanded the order and insisted that Fremont follow the provisions of the First Confiscation Act. Frederick Douglass ridiculed the Lincoln administration for trying to "whip the slaveholders without seriously hurting them."[32] Other African Americans promptly challenged what they perceived to be the inconsistencies in Lincoln's views regarding constitutional limitations. B. K. Sampson charged that on the one hand the president had suspended the writ of habeas corpus in Maryland and allowed Fremont's imposition of martial law in Missouri, yet curiously, he could not find justification for embracing Fremont's proclamation that attempted to destroy the very institution that was undermining the nation. In his actions involving civil liberties, the president had "transcended the constitution," a recognized necessity under certain circumstances. "[I]f in time of war [the Constitution] is transcended in one instance, why not in another...?" Sampson questioned.[33]

When in May 1862, Lincoln countermanded a second general's attempt at emancipation, black Americans' hopes reached a nadir. In late April, General David Hunter, Commander of the Department of the South, proclaimed martial law in the areas under his jurisdiction; a short time later, he followed with a grant of freedom to all enslaved people there.[34] Doubtless fearful, as usual, that he would lose the border states, Lincoln issued a declaration of his own in which he asserted that "neither General Hunter, nor any other commander, or person, has been authorized by the Government of the United States to make proclamations declaring the slaves of any State free."[35] African Americans swiftly condemned this latest attack on freedom. In a Fourth of July address to residents of Yates County,

[32] "The Real Peril of the Republic," *Douglass' Monthly* (October 1861).
[33] Ibid.
[34] Quarles, *Lincoln and the Negro*, 72-73.
[35] "Proclamation Revoking General Hunter's Order of Military Emancipation of May 9, 1862," in Basler, ed., *Collected Works*, 5:222-23.

New York, Frederick Douglass excoriated the president not
only for this most recent affront, but for his prosecution of the
war in general. Citing a host of transgressions—including,
refusing to arm the slaves, declare complete emancipation, and
allowing fugitives for a time to be returned to owners—
Douglass charged,

> An administration without a policy is confessedly an
> administration without brains...we have a right to hold
> Abraham Lincoln sternly responsible for any disaster or
> failure attending the suppression of this rebellion. I
> hold that the rebels can do us no serious harm unless it
> is done through the culpable weakness, imbecility or
> unfaithfulness of those who are charged with the high
> duty, of seeing that the Supreme Law of the land is
> everywhere enforced and obeyed...Lincoln and his
> Cabinet...have fought the rebels with the Olive branch.
> The people must teach them to fight them with the
> sword.[36]

Lincoln's revocation of Hunter's decree especially rankled
black Americans because the president's actions seemingly
slowed the momentum toward emancipation that resulted from
Lincoln's own 6 March 1862, message to Congress recom-
mending that it adopt a joint resolution cooperating with any
state that started a program of gradual emancipation, and from
Congress' abolition of slavery in the District of Columbia.
Under the President's plan, the states would receive "pecuniary
aid" to be used to compensate slaveholders for the loss of their
property.[37] The move had surprised African Americans who
hailed it as "an event which sent a thrill of joy throughout the
North and will meet with hearty response throughout Christen-
dom." Despite Congress' failure to pass the measure, blacks

---

[36] "The Slaveholders' Rebellion (A Speech delivered on the 4th day
of July, at Himrods Corners, Yates Co., N.Y.)," *Douglass' Monthly*
(August 1862).
[37] Basler, ed., *Collected Works*, 5:144-46.

believed that it had secured for Lincoln a "confidence and admiration...such as no man has enjoyed in the present era."[38]

Congress' abolition of slavery in the District of Columbia a few weeks later increased the optimism of African Americans even more. Although Washington's emancipation directly affected only a small number of slaves, blacks embraced it as the beginning of universal freedom. Celebrations extended beyond the nation's capital to other cities of the North where African Americans held huge gatherings and gave thanks for the partial realization of their goal.[39]

At Shiloh Presbyterian Church in New York, Henry Highland Garnet celebrated with members of his congregation as well. But Garnet felt obliged to temper his joy because of a provision in the law for emigration of the newly emancipated, a measure Lincoln had encouraged and supported.[40] Garnet considered colonization "the most ridiculous idea of the times to suppose that men who had watered their native soil with the sweat of their unpaid labor should not cling to its beauties and taste its benefits when freedom came." [41]

Of course, colonization had been embraced by some members of the African American community long before Lincoln proposed it. As laws were passed to proscribe black freedom more completely during the antebellum period, some free people of color sought a more amicable environment outside of the United States. By the 1850s Martin Delany, James T. Holly, and even Garnet, showed favorable regard for the possibility of establishing colonies in Haiti or Central America. On the eve of the war, the British-born emigrationist James Redpath–whom Thomas Hamilton once referred to disdainfully as "an Anglo-Saxon with, at present, Anglo-African proclivi-

[38] "The Emancipation Message," *Weekly Anglo-African* (New York), 22 March 1862.
[39] "Emancipation in Washington," *Weekly Anglo-African* (New York), 26 April 1862.
[40] For indication of Lincoln's satisfaction with the colonization clause in the act abolishing slavery in the District of Columbia, see "Message to Congress," 16 April 1862, in Basler, ed., *Collected Works*, 5:192.
[41] "Religious Rejoicing Over the Emancipation Act at Shiloh Church," *Weekly Anglo-African* (New York), 26 April 1862.

ties"–had established the Haytian Emigration Bureau as a means of recruiting African-Americans for settlement in the island. Redpath secured the bureau's "agents" from among some of the leading men of the black community: H. Ford Douglas, Henry Highland Garnet, William Wells Brown, James T. Holly and others. From week to week *Pine and Palm*, the organization's newspaper, regaled readers with reports from Haiti, "…where neither laws, nor prejudice, nor historical memories press cruelly on persons of African descent; where the people whom America degrades and drives from her are rulers, judges, and generals,…authors, artists, and legislators."[42] Yet, Redpath's efforts met with stiff resistance from most African Americans. When in late 1862, his Haytian Emigration Bureau closed and *Pine and Palm* stopped publication, blacks who were opposed to emigration greeted the news with great satisfaction.[43]

Although emigration efforts had never received significant support from the black community, Lincoln convinced himself that colonization was the most sensible solution to the problem of two incompatible races attempting to share common ground. As early as 3 December 1861, he had recommended to Congress that it make provisions for the colonization of those enslaved persons entering the Union lines under the stipulations of the First Confiscation Act. He suggested as well (much to the dismay of free blacks) that Congress might consider "whether the free colored people already in the United States could not, as far as individuals may desire, be included in such colonization."[44] Predictably, African Americans responded indignantly:

---

[42] Quoted in McPherson, *The Negro's Civil War*, 78.

[43] See *Douglass' Monthly* (November 1862). Douglass expressed his contempt for Redpath and his activities, indicating that he was glad the emigrationist had "ceased to exert his talents in the cause of…colonization." See the *Weekly Anglo-African* (New York), 29 March 1862, for a candid reply to questions about Redpath's ethnicity and "Anglo-African proclivities." Quoted from Lincoln's First Inaugural Address, in Basler, ed., *Collected Works*, 4:250. Lincoln had initially made the remark in Ottawa, Illinois on 21 August 1858, as the first in a series of debates with the incumbent senator.

[44] "Annual Message to Congress," 3 December 1861, in Basler, ed., *Collected Works*, 4:48

As free colored men, we thank Mr. Lincoln for nothing, when he asks Congress to provide for the expatriation of such of us as may be desirous to leave the country. We are decidedly of the opinion that we will stay: any surplus change Congress may have can be appropriated "with our consent" to expatriate and settle elsewhere the surviving slaveholders.[45]

When little had come of his suggestion by the summer of 1862, Lincoln decided to take his solution for racial incompatibility to the black community directly. Rather than meet with the African American leadership, however, he chose on 14 August to invite to the White House a committee of five men virtually unknown to the national black community.[46] Once assembled, Lincoln provided the group with reasons why the two races could not coexist in America, citing the physical differences between them as "a great disadvantage to us both, as I think your race suffer very greatly, many of them by living among us, while ours suffer from your presence." Having given what he obviously considered a logical argument for emigration, Lincoln proceeded to outline his plans for African American economic success in a foreign land.[47]

The black community was no more interested in this latest move to coax them out of the country of their birth than any of Lincoln's earlier attempts. A staunch anti-emigrationist, Frederick Douglass ridiculed Lincoln who "assumes the language and arguments of an itinerant Colonization lecturer, showing all his inconsistencies, his pride of race and blood, his con-tempt for Negroes and his canting hypocrisy."[48] In response to Lincoln's suggestion that white men were fighting each other because of black men, Douglass made the now-famous retort:

---

[45] "The President's Message," *Weekly Anglo-African* (NewYork), 7 December 1861.

[46] Benjamin Quarles indicates that four of the five men had recently acquired their freedom. See Quarles, *Lincoln and the Negro*, 115-16.

[47] Basler, ed., *Collected Works*, 5:370-75. Lincoln envisioned black emigration to Central America where African-Americans could find employment in, among other things, the coal mines.

[48] "The President and His Speeches," *Douglass' Monthly* (September 1862).

It is not the innocent horse that makes the horse thief,
not the traveler's purse that makes the high-way robber, and it is not the presence of the negro that causes
this foul and unnatural war, but the cruel and brutal
cupidity of those who wish to possess horses, money
and Negroes by means of theft, robbery and rebellion.[49]

[handwritten margin note: emancipation proclamation]

African Americans could hardly have guessed that the man
proposing black emigration was about to place into motion a
plan of universal emancipation of enslaved people in the Confederate South. Although they had been vociferously pressing
for it since the beginning of the war, Lincoln's preliminary
proclamation caught black people by surprise.

As pleased as they were, however, people of color
recognized the need for continued vigilance in the struggle for
emancipation. In an address aimed at European supporters of
freedom, Douglass warned that "...the end is not yet...The
pledge of Emancipation rests upon a contingency. We on our
part should leave nothing to contingency, but work steadily to
keep the public mind and heart up to the one grand object,
until it shall become an accomplished fact."[50]

When the final proclamation took effect on 1 January 1863,
African Americans proclaimed victory. Nonetheless, they recognized the limitations of the document–slaves from the border
states and those from areas under Union occupation were ex-
cluded from its provisions; and it was, as one observer put it,
"...no more humanitarian than a hundred pounder rifled cannon," in that both sought to deprive the South of a very valuable labor force. But blacks also believed that the large number
of those freed by its provisions ensured the eventual freedom of
the rest.[51]

And so it was. With the Emancipation Proclamation, the war
became what African Americans always felt it should be. Black
liberation had become a necessary by-product of the conflict.

[49] Ibid.
[50] "Address to Our Readers and Friends in Great Britain and
Ireland," *Douglass' Monthly* (October 1862).
[51] *Weekly Anglo-African* (New York), 3 January 1863.

The cold, practical motivations for Lincoln's actions meant less to blacks than the favorable consequences. At no time, however, did black abolitionists forget the slowness by which he moved toward emancipation, or his support for colonization. When they met in national convention in October 1864, they thanked Lincoln, his cabinet, and Congress for the measures that had been implemented which favored African Americans; but they pointed as well to the many disabilities that continued to circumscribe their lives. Most illuminating of all, perhaps, was their suggestion that despite recent developments (the Emancipation Proclamation included), African Americans continued to have "painful doubt and apprehension" concerning their ultimate status. They warned that if the North attempted to reconstruct the Union with slavery intact, blacks would regard this as a "flagrant violation of good faith on the part of the Government, false to the brave colored men who have fallen in its defense, unjust to the living who are periling their lives for its protection, and to be resisted by the whole moral power of the civilized world."[52]

Fundamental differences had separated the thinking of Lincoln and his black critics. From the perspective of African Americans, the war had been clear cut. It was one of patriot against traitor, freedom instead of bondage, right overcoming wrong. Lincoln's views on constitutional limitations, his concerns over securing the loyalty of the border states, his personal connections with the South, and finally his nineteenth century racial attitudes, all shaped his policy toward the Confederate states and enslaved blacks. African American abolitionists, conversely, were compelled—in many instances by their own memories of enslavement and by their quest for equality—to reject any action that fell short of emancipation. They insisted that Lincoln be an abolitionist; conciliation, moderation, caution, they believed, would endanger the cause of freedom. Given his set of imperatives, however, he could never have been what African Americans wished. Certainly, on some level they

---

[52] Howard Holman Bell, ed., *Minutes of the Proceedings of the National Negro Conventions, 1830-1864* (New York: Arno Press and the New York Times, 1969) 34, 51.

understood that. Yet, that recognition did not deter them from pressing for universal emancipation or from criticizing Lincoln when he seemingly hindered the realization of that goal. From the black perspective, any risks they took were reasonable, given the long-term consequences of inaction. "We have our all at stake," Jermain Loguen had declared, "hence something more than the mere 'Union' to fight for[;] that, with Slavery, is to us worse than nothing."[53]

[53] J. W. Loguen's letter to the editor, *Weekly Anglo-African* (New York), 14 September 1861.

6

WHY BOOTH SHOT LINCOLN

By Terry Alford

On Saturday, 15 April 1865, William Warren, a popular comedian, was on the afternoon train from Manchester, New Hampshire, to Boston. The conductor suddenly appeared in the aisle and announced "the news of the horrid murder of Abraham Lincoln by John Wilkes Booth." Warren was astonished. He had always thought John Booth the brightest and cleverest of the family. He did not believe what he was hearing. Therefore, he stood up and contradicted the conductor. "Flatly" contradicted him, Warren wrote in his diary; "but, alas," he added, "it proved too true."[1]

William Warren may be forgiven his surprise at the news. Many other people acquainted with John Wilkes Booth were equally astonished. "It is a strange thing if [Booth] be guilty of this crime," one New York City editor wrote immediately after the assassination. "He is a young fellow of spirit, of acute mind, and of great professional vigor... His temperament is romantic and poetical. His disposition has been considered as gentle. There are neither circumstances nor antecedents... to mark him as a man likely to conceive or execute such a crime... His complicity in such a conspiracy appears to astound all who knew him."[2] A friend of Booth's from Illinois agreed, writing

---

[1] Asia B. Clarke, *John Wilkes Booth: A Sister's Memoir*, ed. Terry Alford (Jackson: 1996) X.
[2] Unidentified New York City newspaper, April 1865, Carrington scrapbook, John Hay Library, Brown University.

he was not aware that Booth "could kill Lincoln or any other man."[3]

All who knew him knew he had those elements of audacity and determination necessary for bold acts, but they "never thought he had the murderous heart, the moral poltroonery, and the inexpressible wickedness which stamps the assassin as the vilest of God's creatures," stated the editor of a theatrical newspaper.[4]

Why did John Wilkes Booth do it? Why did he murder Abraham Lincoln? As Benjamin Franklin wisely observed, "men and melons are hard to know." There are features of Booth's life and personality that fly in the face of the customary profile of an assassin. He was professionally successful, popular, well-liked, even admired by many. No loner, he had an army of friends, and his ability to charm and attract the opposite sex was legendary. He is, in other words, a person with something to lose, not a born loser.

An essential first step to understanding the assassination is to keep in mind its wartime context. "The times–they seem to be sadly out of joint," wrote a South Carolina editor in 1862. "The nations of the earth are shaking. We are in the midst of revolutions."[5] It is not possible to understand the murder outside the war that produced it. Can anyone imagine Booth shooting poor old President Garfield or the inconsequential President McKinley? The assassination was provoked by Northern victory in the war. With very good reason, it occurred at the very climax of the war.

It would take some time to list fully what Lincoln's opponents would term the oppressive and unconstitutional measures of his government. They were revolutionary changes, representing an unprecedented expansion of federal power. Any such list would include the first national draft, taking of hostages, confiscation of property, arrests without trials, trials by military commission, travel and trade restrictions, the income tax, and of course, emancipation. Merely expressing outrage at

[3] *Cincinnati Commercial Gazette*, 24 January 1891.
[4] *Play Bill*, 21 April 1865.
[5] *The Southern Presbyterian*, 18 January 1862.

the abolition nature of the war had gotten some Northerners arrested in the fall of 1862. "Present address, Fort Warren [Prison]," one Marylander wrote at that time; "Future address, unknown."[6] Merrill Peterson, in his book *Lincoln in American Memory*, reminds us that to Lincoln, the preservation of the nation justified the emergency exercise of whatever powers proved necessary.

Some contemporaries disagreed. In an anonymous letter written from New York after the assassination, a writer informed President Andrew Johnson that "Abraham Lincoln was killed because he was [a] usurper, and trampled upon the laws of the country, because he took away the security of the citizen and tramped our magna charta [sic] in the dust. The last words of the noble hearted but misguided Boothe [sic] were not the utterances of a vile murderer, but were the breathings of one who loved his country, and was determined that no beast of 'brief authority' should trample on its Constitution and live."[7]

Whatever one might think of the intelligence of this writer, he was smart enough not to sign his own name. He signed, instead, the name of *New York Tribune* editor Horace Greeley. The actual author of the letter is unknown. But the letter's sentiments, if not its signature, would have been willingly endorsed by countless conservative and reactionary Northerners and Border State residents. Mark Neely, in his fine book *The Fate of Liberty: Abraham Lincoln and Civil Liberties*, informs us that the Lincoln government made no truly systematic attempt to suppress the free speech of this group in the North. Its episodic attempts were effective enough, apparently, in showing where the line was drawn and cautioning critics. Mounting military successes did an even better job at stemming dissent.

Admitting Lincoln's ambition and his single-mindedness, he still seems today more scrupulous, more compassionate, and far-sighted than the majority of his allies. Yet these facts are plain, too. He looked dangerous to his critics. Josephine Seaton, daughter of the founding editor of the *National Intelligencer*

---

6 *Baltimore Sun*, 7 June 1903.
7 New York City, 9 October 1865, in Baker Files, Turner-Baker Papers, M-797, National Archives.

newspaper, wrote to former President James Buchanan, that in her eyes he (Buchanan) would be the last constitutional president the nation would ever have. If it were not Lincoln's own doing, her letter implies, the times would push Lincoln, or someone like Lincoln forward.[8] Her father's conservative peers in the editorial business had already cautioned readers that civil wars in European history often ended in dictatorships.

W. P. Davis shared her gloom. An Indiana Democratic Party leader, Davis wrote in 1864, "We will never...have another presidential election. [Lincoln] will be proclaimed Emperor long before his term expires...It will be what a majority of the people want, what they absolutely need, and what they will get."[9]

More than half of American voters in 1860 wanted someone other than Abraham Lincoln for president. Millions considered his election a calamity for the country. A large portion of these millions were willing to form an alternative government rather than submit to his. They were ready to fight a devastating war to stay clear of him. Hundreds of thousands of Americans hated him cordially. Thousands made personal threats against him. Hundreds must have fantasized doing him in. A handful actually conspired to make attacks upon him. However, in a nation of thirty-two million people, only one individual—John Wilkes Booth—stepped up to him and pulled the trigger.

Booth shared many of the antipathies to Lincoln that the great president's other opponents did. But what were some of those special characteristics that made Booth unique in his terrifying combination of motive and will? Why Booth, and only Booth, out of the vast sea of the American people?

At Dr. Samuel A. Mudd's trial in 1865, Mudd's defending attorney said, "Booth was ...intelligent, agreeable, of attractive manner, with no known [disabling] blemish on his character as a man or a citizen. His society, so far from being shunned, was courted, and the fairest ladies of the land, the daughters of distinguished statesmen and patriots, deemed it no dispar-

---

[8] William E. Ames, *A History of the National Intelligencer* (Chapel Hill: 1972) 332.

[9] W. P. Davis to John G. Davis, 24 October 1864, quoted in L. L. Sylvester, "Oliver P. Morton and Hoosier Politics During the Civil War," (Ph.D. diss., Indiana University, 1968) 282.

agement to them to accept his escort and his attentions. It is not extravagant to say that hundreds of true, Union-loving people, in [Washington, DC] and other cities, were on terms of cordial and intimate association with him. And why should they not have been?"[10] This is indeed John Wilkes Booth. It is no veneer. He was a handsome, winning fellow. And yet, it is not the complete individual.

It might be interesting to consider for a moment what college students read about Booth. For the last several years, I have collected accounts of the Lincoln assassination from the principal college-level American History textbooks. A publisher's representative shared his company product manual that identified the fifteen leading textbooks, all of which I examined. What do college students read in these texts? (Or should I say what are they assigned to read there? Believe it or not, I feel occasionally that some actually neglect to do it.)

Textbooks routinely give about a paragraph, or even a half-paragraph, to the assassination. As a quick check to an author's attention to detail, I always look first to see if the name of Ford's Theatre is correctly spelled. Less than half of the texts do so. One author terms "Our American Cousin" a new comedy. It had been around for years. Only one takes the space to quote from an eyewitness account.

As for Booth, we read the following:

— Houghton-Mifflin: an embittered Southern sympathizer
— Harper Collins: a Southern sympathizer
— Prentice Hall: a Confederate sympathizer
— Wadsworth: an actor and Confederate sympathizer

One is forced to conclude at this point that Booth was a highly sympathetic person.

In 1874 Booth's sister, Asia Clarke, completed a manuscript about her brother. This odd but loving memoir was published in book form in 1938. It is a very imperfect book in some

---

10 *Baltimore Sun*, 8 July 1934.

respects. Nevertheless, it contains some profound observations on the future assassin.[11]

Her brother was not a quick learner, Asia writes. He was insecure about his abilities in that regard and once termed himself a "dullard." He had, in compensation, an ability to concentrate and a dogged persistence. Asia thought he possessed what she terms "a tenacious rather than [an] intuitive intelligence" like his brothers.

Two exceedingly interesting features of personality are noted next. One was a certain "quality of combativeness." "From early boyhood he was argumentative and fervid in debate." He was remorseless, and "he would wear his argument threadbare." His discussion of things was didactic. These traits were combined with an ardent and impulsive nature, which was sometimes thoughtless of consequences.

The second feature of Booth is not merely interesting, it is portentous. Asia was struck by the way in which her brother would imagine challenges as individual opponents. These he would then attack with a military spirit. A list of tough spelling words, for example, he might set up mentally as a battalion of enemy soldiers. By doing what Asia terms "individualizing" (or personalizing) a problem into a human adversary, Booth told his sister, "I always come out in victory." Pretending something is "a reality in form and life," as he put it, "I lay my demon."

By Booth's teenage years the love of politics had grown passionate. "Long arguments followed the slightest divergence into politics," his sister wrote, "for he loved argument and disputation...More than once [he} made me late for meals ...through the desire to 'clinch an argument.'" During this period Asia also noted a class-consciousness in her brother. It was unbecoming, "undemocratic" in her opinion. Happily this feeling was transient as it was one thing truly out of Booth's nature. It was also out of place in a family with as little money as his.

[11] Clarke's reminiscences of her brother were originally published under the title *The Unlocked Book: A Memoir of John Wilkes Booth by His Sister* (New York: 1938). A new edition with relevant family documents and an index was published in 1996 and is cited in note 1.

In the mid-1850s Booth supported Maryland's vibrant Know-Nothing Party. Asia's book contains a few passionate complaints by her brother about Irish immigrants enlisting in the Union army during the war years. "Nothing grated this fierce Southern partisan so sorely as beholding the easy enlistment of Irishmen," she claimed. Booth complained to his sister that it was degrading to the nation to see how anxious these immigrants were to fight for the freedom of the slaves. If these indeed be his feelings, it is curious they are not prominently mentioned by other people besides his sister. Perhaps these are only her feelings. Asia was not free of anti-Irish prejudice. But, if accurately described, these prejudices did not prevent Booth from forming friendships with Irish and Irish-Americans. One of his closest friends was the Irish-born actor John McCullough.

In 1859 Booth was present as a soldier at the execution of abolitionist John Brown in Charlestown, (West) Virginia. Booth despised abolitionists. This point cannot be made too strongly. It is one of the most consistent features of his political philosophy. He felt that they had "slain us" as a nation when they agitated the sectional problem into war fever. Brown deserved no mercy. "I may say I helped to hang John Brown and while I live, I shall think with joy of the day I saw the sun go down upon one traitor less without our land."

In Brown, Booth found something to admire as well as to hate, however. Brown was a worthy enemy, better than his antislavery peers, because he was a man of direct action. He did not employ the subterfuge other abolitionists used to maneuver the South into secession. Brown's "treason was no more than theirs," Booth wrote of these abolitionists in 1860,"[and perhaps less so] for open force is holier than hidden craft. The lion is more noble than the fox."[12]

One reads with interest these remarks of Booth's, made more than four years before the murder of President Lincoln. They are a curious mixture of sentiments. Booth feels Brown died as he should have for bringing violent abolitionism to

[12] John Rhodehamel and Louise Taper, eds., *"Right or Wrong, God Judge Me:" The Writings of John Wilkes Booth* (Urbana and Chicago: University of Illinois Press, 1997) 60.

John Wilkes Booth
(Courtesy of *The Abraham Lincoln Museum*)

Virginia. Yet, because he was a man of open action and not of stealth, he was more praiseworthy than those cowardly preachers who attacked slavery from the safety of Northern pulpits.

In an 1864 letter known as the "To Whom It May Concern", Booth was still being compelled by Brown. This letter shows Booth's awareness of the desperate situation of the rebel states and his deep sense of anger and betrayal at the loss of the pre-war Union. Brown again came to mind. Booth writes, "What was a crime in poor John Brown is now considered (by [the Republican Party]), as the greatest and only virtue. Strange transmigration! Vice to become virtue simply because more indulge in it. I thought then, as now, that the abolitionists were the only traitors in the land, and that the entire party deserve the same fate as poor old Brown; not because they wish to abolish slavery, but on account of the means they have ever endeavored to use to effect that abolition. If Brown were living, I doubt whether he himself would set slavery against the Union."[13]

George Alfred Townsend, a journalist quite knowledgeable about details of Booth's life, was quick to see a connection between the Brown raid and the Lincoln assassination. Booth, he felt, "took from the scene [of Brown's execution] inspiration enough to slay a merciful president in his unsuspecting leisure." Townsend knew that Booth did not take Brown's death lightly. He "never referred to [it] in bravado," but–profoundly impressed–he "may have learned his mode" of warfare from the militant abolitionist.[14] "John Brown was a man inspired," Booth told Asia, "the grandest character of this century."

Booth did not enlist in the Confederate army when the war broke out, and that was a grave personal mistake for him. The story that he promised his mother not to do so seems genuine. He felt an intense sense of obligation for his mother. Beyond that, the Booth family situation may help explain his decision. His mother was a widow. She lived with his semi-invalid sister.

---

[13] Clarke, *John Wilkes Booth*, 108.
[14] George A. Townsend, *The Life, Crime, and Capture of John Wilkes Booth* (New York: 1865) 22.

Money was not abundant. Son Junius had been absent for years in California. Son Edwin was leaving for Europe. Son Joseph was erratic, a worry to the family, and soon to depart on a round-the-world trip. Who, then, was to help her? Accordingly, Booth stayed out of the army.

And he stayed north during the war, performing on no Confederate stage. He understood that, in a general way, the price of performing in the North was keeping his mouth as shut as possible. He never concealed completely his political views–he could not have done so–"but, at the same time," as a police reporter wrote in 1865, "unless under the influence of liquor ...he avoided the discussion of public questions [with casual acquaintances] and was [wary] in the expression of his sentiments except among his...friends."[15] Nothing could have been worse for the young idealist. As a friend in Albany, New York, observed, "His sentiments only grew stronger for repression."[16]

Booth lost no immediate family members in the fighting of the Civil War. A first cousin died of battle wounds in 1864, however. We have no account of his reaction to this event, but we do know that Booth had been fond of the cousin's family and must have felt badly for and with them. The death at Union hands of two Southerners whom he knew greatly upset him, all the more so because both men were prisoners and hence defenseless. One was Jessie Wharton, a friend and school-mate. Wharton was shot to death by a prison guard in 1862.[17] Early in 1865, John Yates Beall, a Virginian whom Booth had known at the time of the Brown raid, was executed for conducting sabotage and irregular warfare in the North. Beall's death occurred less than two months before the assassination.[18] A friend of Booth's heard him denounce the president in the bitterest of terms for allowing the execution to be carried out.

[15] *National Police Gazette*, 22 April 1865.

[16] H. P. Phelps, *Players of a Century. A Record of the Albany Stage* (New York: 1972) 326.

[17] John A. Marshall, *American Bastille* (Philadelphia: 1870) 342-343.

[18] William A. Tidwell, *April '65: Confederate Covert Action in the American Civil War* (Kent OH and London: 1995) 145.

The legend that built up about the Booth-Beall relationship blames Secretary of State William Seward, as well as Lincoln, for the death. It is not widely recalled today just how despised William Seward was by the conservative element of the nation. Lincoln's secretary of state had been early and long active in the anti-slavery interest. By 1860 he was as intensely disliked as Lincoln by those on the Southern side, maybe more so. Seward was particularly obnoxious to Booth for the role he played in the pacification of Maryland at the start of the war. Pro-Southern Marylanders blamed Seward for the arrests of the Lincoln opposition that broke the back of the state's rebel movement in the summer of 1861.

Booth was particularly incensed at the arrest of George P. Kane of Baltimore. Kane, the city's marshal, was arrested at 3:00 A.M. on a June morning in 1861. Kane, and Booth, blamed Seward for Kane's lengthy incarceration. As Kane put it, "All that is bad in a man, unpatriotic in a citizen, and corrupt in an officer finds itself concentrated in this individual."[19]

During an 1862 appearance in New York City, Booth had stayed clear of political arguments. He had listened attentively to angry discussions between cast members, but from himself "not a word of politics was ever heard" for nearly a week. When Kane's name was mentioned, however, Booth exploded, "I know George P. Kane well; he is my friend, and the man who could draft him from the bosom of his family for no crime whatever, but a mere suspicion that he may commit one some time, deserves a dog's death." The words were impressive, but what most struck the person who recorded them was the powerful emotion with which Booth delivered them.[20] Here, before the war was one year old, Booth was already outraged at the actions of Lincoln's government.

Over the years a number of personal traits have been advanced traditionally to explain the assassination. For instance,

[19] Ralph W. Powell, "George Proctor Kane: Hero or Traitor?," (paper presented at the First Annual Honors' Student History Conference, Northern Virginia Community College, Annandale, VA, 21 April 1990) 19.

[20] Gordon Samples, *Lust for Fame: The Stage Career of John Wilkes Booth* (Jefferson NC and London: 1982) 170.

almost every historical writer has agreed on one point–that Booth had an excessive desire for fame. They draw this notion from a number of 1865 accounts, like that given by a Booth acquaintance who worked on the Washington and Baltimore Railroad. According to this person, Booth told him several weeks before the murder that he [Booth] wanted to "do something which the world would remember for all time."[21]

Though Booth had the desire that any young person does to distinguish himself from his parents and family, Booth also had a large share of ambition in his profession. This, too, was necessary for success. It is interesting to add the unusual fact, however, that among his most formidable rivals for theatrical fame were older members of the very same family from which, as a youth, he needed to distance himself.

Stage fame is fleeting and it can be purchased only at a great cost of body and mind. The desire to be lastingly famous—to write history and make things happen in a significant way—was native enough to his personality. It was an element in the recipe of 14 April.

Other writers have noted a relationship between Booth's drinking and the assassination. One must be careful in treating this topic, because it is not a neutral one. Preachers and prohibitionists have loved it. It also fits into a certain abolitionist theme about the morally dissipated Southern character. No surprise for them that Mrs. Surratt kept a tavern! How appropriate! "Liquor was abundant at every step of the plot for the killing of the president, " wrote Charles T. White in his 1921 book *Lincoln and Prohibition.* "John Wilkes Booth, the arch assassin, well stimulated himself with liquor shortly before he fired the fatal shot."

Alcohol played an important and destructive role in the life of Booth's father. As a young man, Booth was both attracted and frightened to death by it. One may say he was, as a friend claims, "born to a taste for liquor."[22] This taste was termed "the family failing" by a friendly and admiring old actress. Booth struggled with this failing successfully at times. He was not a

[21] *New York Clipper,* 29 April 1865.
[22] *New York Telegraph,* 23 May 1909.

barroom loafer, as Jenny Gourlay of Ford's Theatre notes correctly.[23] He was active, intelligent and successful. And he never disgraced himself by appearing drunk on stage as his father had done.

But Booth admitted to a friend in the spring of 1865 that he had "the blues." Like many another person with the blues, he found some solace in the depressant and anesthetizing qualities of alcohol.

Unhappily for Booth, drinking "brought out the bandit in him," as one acquaintance noted. It was an accelerator, not a brake. Actor John McCullough, who knew him as well as anyone outside his immediate family, always believed that liquor enhanced a certain volatility in Booth. The role of liquor is referred to by every writer on the assassination, but has it been carefully considered? Was it true, as Booth's friend Harry Langdon observed, "Whiskey had a great deal to do with the murder..."[24]

A third traditional explanation of the murder is that Booth was insane. He was not insane in any obvious sense. He organized an actual conspiracy directed at least two other government leaders besides Lincoln. This shows a method to his actions and a political nature to his crime. And there are other signs. He thought hard about the adverse consequences of his actions. He knew what ill effect it would have on himself and his family. He was aware it would bring misery (his word) to them. He was cautious, generally, in his planning. He gave considerable thought to his escape and showed at all times a strong desire to live through the consequences of his action.

Booth could be eccentric and moody. He could be reckless, easily bored and intimidating to friends. There was a quirk in him, said a Ford's Theatre friend. For nearly two years some had noted an increased absent-mindedness and volatility. There were periods by the spring of 1865 when he was unable to sleep regularly. He was often depressed and further troubled by an on-again, off-again relationship with his fiancée. He was

---

[23] *Minneapolis Journal*, 27 April 1914.
[24] Harry Langdon, interview by George A. Townsend, (1883), photocopy in author's collection.

incensed by the displays of triumph shown in the capital when Richmond was captured. Hay and Nicolay, biographers of Lincoln, felt that with Lee's surrender, there came to Booth "an access of malice and rage akin to madness."[25] "I can't see why there should be such great rejoicing...," he told someone. "What I want, and I am as good a Union man as anyone, is peace."[26] The day before the murder he announced that he felt a little desperate.

In her memoir, Asia Booth had recalled her brother's political fever as the war's shadows began to lengthen against the South. No theme stood out so much as his anxiety that Lincoln might become a king. "No, by God's mercy," he once cried, springing to his feet. "Never that!" A Bonaparte, a king, a reign...all words which fell from his lips. These were no discussions. These thoughts were expressed in what Asia terms "wild tirades [springing] from a distracted brain and tortured heart."[27] Asia was worried about him.

It is curious how, in dynamic historical moments, events focus around an individual and push that person forward from a leader to a symbol, to something larger than life. Events had done this to Abraham Lincoln, and Booth "individualized" (to borrow his sister's term) Lincoln as the cause of the nation's woes. "Our country owed all our troubles to him" Booth wrote in his diary after the murder.

In reading the Booth interviews given by A. W. Smiley, one is highly impressed with just this point. Booth had grown close to Smiley, a friend made in the Pennsylvania oil country in 1864. Smiley was struck by Booth's personal antagonism to Lincoln. "[Booth] never said anything on the subject of the armed controversy between North and South" to Smiley. But his feelings against the Northern president were intense and unmistakable. Months before the murder, Smiley knew clearly "from [Booth's] utterances that he had a very strong hatred of Abe Lincoln." "I would rather have my right arm cut off at the

---

[25] J. G. Nicolay and John Hay, "The Fourteenth of April," *Century Magazine* (January 1890): 433.
[26] "The Assassination," undated clipping in Booth scrapbook, Folger Shakespeare Library, Washington, DC.
[27] Clarke, *John Wilkes Booth,* 82-89.

shoulder than see Lincoln made president again," he told Smiley.[28] No wonder he stalked Lincoln on inauguration day in 1865. According to actor E. A. Emerson, Lincoln had become Booth's obsession by 14 April 1865.[29]

When the Indiana Democrat W. P. Davis reflected upon the possibility of a Lincoln kingship, he did so with grim fatalism. "It is what [the American people's] capacity requires. They have not, nor never had, sense nor honesty enough to maintain a republican form of government. Hence, a limited monarchy will suit them much better. It is, in fact, as good as they deserve," Davis wrote bitterly.[30]

Unlike Davis, Booth embraced no such fatalism. Like Davis, he felt the American people had grown degenerate. But unlike Davis, he could never resign himself to the defeat of his own views. As his sister noted, "He was a man so single in his devotion, so unswerving in his principles that he would yield everything for the cause he espoused." Reflecting on one encounter with her brother, she saw a terrifying consistency in him. "I knew he was today what he had been from childhood," she stated.[31]

Lincoln knew precisely to what such obsessions could lead. Oddly enough, he learned it by watching the abolitionists. "An enthusiast broods over the oppression of a people till he fancies himself commissioned by Heaven to liberate them," Lincoln once said. "He ventures the attempt, which ends in little else than his own execution."[32] Lincoln was speaking of John Brown, but one can see how clearly the worlds apply to John Wilkes Booth as well.

The actual shooting of Lincoln is not my topic. Accounts of it are abundant in the newspapers of 1865. One also reads there

[28] Ernest C. Miller, *John Wilkes Booth in the Pennsylvania Oil Region* (Warren PA: 1987) 72.

[29] Undated clipping "April Fourteenth 1865," scrapbook, 43, McLellan Collection, John Hay Library, Brown University.

[30] Sylvester, "O. P. Morton," 282.

[31] Clarke, *John Wilkes Booth*, 83.

[32] James Stevenson, "Romantic Glimpses of Abraham Lincoln," *Lincoln Herald*, 90 (Fall 1988): 103, citing Basler, ed., *Collected Works*, 3:541.

the almost inexpressible shock, anger, and sorrow of millions of people.

For fresh perspectives on the assassination, I often turn to foreign newspapers. In some way, their distance in miles and culture is not dissimilar from our own distance today from events of that night. They are able to see it without being it. From the foreign press two observations stand out as especially insightful.

The *Toronto Leader* wondered, on hearing the terrible news from Washington, about the inner nature of the assassin. "There must have been a strong feeling on the part of the person who committed the crime that a grievous wrong had been done, either to himself or to his country, by the president or the government he represented... He must have been goaded almost to the verge of madness."

Another foreign newspaper touched on the motive of revenge. This element should never be forgotten in analyzing the assassination. Two Washington diarists noted on 15 April that Booth cried "Vengeance for the South" or "The South avenged." Two eyewitnesses who wrote letters on 15 April, and one who wrote on 16 April, also report Booth's shout of vengeance. A soldier named Sheldon McIntyre, who was present at the theatre, wrote on 8 May that Booth cried, "Revenge for the South." Likewise, James P. Ferguson, testifying at the conspiracy trial, stated he heard the words, "Revenge for the South."[33]

Revenge returns one perceived injury for another. Most of us would conclude it makes poor public policy. But it is often a compelling human motive. The London *Illustrated News* wrote, "It is no idle phrase to say that the news [of Lincoln's assassination] sent a shudder to the great heart of a people." One could say in response–exactly!

The actual causes of the Lincoln murder reside at the juncture of Booth's unique personality and the Confederate collapse in 1865. It was, as Booth's best friend John McCullough ob-

---

[33] Timothy S. Good, ed., *We Saw Lincoln Shot: One Hundred Eyewitness Accounts* (Jackson: 1995), contains many of the most relevant accounts.

served, no single thing and no sudden impulse. Rather it was the interconnection of "100 queer acts."[34]

"Sic Semper Tyrannis" was a motto of the *Richmond Whig* newspaper. Booth wished to be remembered as the avenger of this ideal–as its Brutus and its William Tell. He did receive a few shouts of acclaim. At a mass meeting held in Shreveport, Louisiana, a Confederate colonel from Texas paid "a glowing panegyric upon Booth...whom he compared to Brutus, the slayer of Caesar, and predicted for [Booth] a like and enduring fame."[35]

But it was not fame that came to Booth in our history. It was infamy. To Lincoln's hard-won titles as victor and humanitarian, the crown of martyrdom could now be added by his admirers. It was handed to them by Lincoln's worst enemy. Booth sank like a dust speck on the opposing scale. Gone was the fine actor, devoted son, and cherished friend. The fanatic and skulking coward replaced it.

Booth brings special meaning to the words of General William Tecumseh Sherman: "War and individual ruin are synonymous terms." On 14 April 1865, Booth laid his demon. To his own astonishment—in the mind of millions of his fellow citizens—he now became one himself.

[34] *Cincinnati Enquirer*, 2 July 1885.
[35] John Barr, "The Tyrannicide's Reception: Texans Respond to Lincoln's Assassination," (M.A. thesis, School of Human Sciences and Humanities, University of Houston, 1988), has a highly interesting third chapter along these lines.

7

SHOOTING THE PRESIDENT AS A MILITARY NECESSITY

By William Hanchett

When Mary Lincoln realized the cause of all the commotion beside her in the box at Ford's Theatre the night of 14 April 1865, an eye-witness reported that she jumped to her feet, waved her arms in the air, and screamed, "They have shot the president."[1] If she did use these words, she was the first to interpret the assassination of Abraham Lincoln as a conspiracy of Confederates, for there was no doubt to whom her pronoun referred. Her quick assumption was the most common and most natural one.

Vice President Andrew Johnson, soon to become president: "They shall suffer for this. They shall suffer for this."

Secretary of the Navy Gideon Welles: "Damn the Rebels. This is their work."

Secretary of War Edwin M. Stanton: The assassination was "deliberately planned and set on foot by rebels, under pretense of avenging the South and aiding the rebel cause."

General Ulysses S. Grant: "Extreme rigor will have to be observed whilst assassination remains the order of the day with the rebels."

The Springfield, Illinois, *Daily State Journal*: The assassination "was the last effort of defeated traitors to

1 Annie F. F. Wright, The Assassination of Abraham Lincoln," *Magazine of History*, 8/2 (February 1909): 113-14.

seize the government and light anew the flames of civil war."[2]

On 2 May, after a frantic investigation by the War Department, President Johnson gave official sanction to the general assumption. It appeared, declared the president, that the "atrocious murder" of Lincoln had been "incited, concerted, and procured" by Jefferson Davis and five Rebel officials operating out of Canada. He offered huge rewards for the arrest of these men.[3]

The man who pulled the trigger, the popular young actor John Wilkes Booth, was killed at the time of his capture on 26 April but in May and June, eight of his associates were tried by a military commission for having conspired the assassination with Booth, Davis, and the others named in the president's proclamation. All were found guilty. Four were sentenced to prison and four were hanged. The government had thus proved that the assassination was a Confederate conspiracy, for if these eight were guilty of having conspired the assassination with Booth and the Confederate leaders, then these latter were guilty of having conspired it with them. But not so fast.

From the first there had been a controversy over the legality of trying the conspirators in a military court, and there were strong misgivings about the haste with which the hangings were carried out. The president approved the sentences on 5 July and the traps were sprung on 7 July. The night before, Lincoln's friend Orville Browning said that since the commission had acted without legal authority, its proceedings were void. "The execution of these persons will be murder." The New York diarist George Templeton Strong wrote of the execution, "It will do us harm....Reaction against this will save Jeff Davis's worthless neck."[4] The reaction to the conspiracy trial

[2] As quoted in Hans Trefousse, *Andrew Johnson* (New York: W. W. Norton, 1989) 194; John Niven, *Gideon Welles* (New York: Oxford University Press, 1973) 492; *Official Records, War of the Rebellion* (hereafter *Official Records*), 46:3:762, 784-5; photocopy of newspaper in James S. Copley Library, San Diego CA.

[3] *Messages and Papers of the President*, 4:307-8.

[4] *Diary of Orville Hickman Browning*, ed. James G. Randall (Springfield: Illinois State Historical Library, 1933) 2:37; *Diary of*

and its findings was strong indeed, so strong that it still affects our thinking about the assassination.

Even while the trial was in progress, some of the government's evidence against the Confederate leaders was challenged as untrustworthy, and soon after it ended the testimony of three principal witnesses was exposed as perjured. In November Stanton withdrew the offer of rewards for the men named in the president's proclamation who were still at large.[5] Radical members of Congress who had talked freely about hangings during the war now began to advocate a peace of Lincolnian magnanimity.[6] The Radical Thaddeus Stevens declared, "I know these men, sir. They are gentlemen and incapable of being assassins," a statement long considered to represent their definitive exoneration.[7] Powerful New York editors like Horace Greeley and Henry J. Raymond joined in the repudiation of the government's case,[8] and within two or three decades public opinion had so shifted that most Americans considered it shameful that US officials had ever even suspected they had shot the president.

Yet not all the testimony at the conspiracy trial incriminating the Confederate leadership was discredited. In *Beware the People Weeping* (1982), the first book on the assassination by a professional historian, Thomas R. Turner states, "Taking away all the testimony that was obviously perjured, there was still a volume of apparently untainted testimony that led to the... conclusion of southern involvement and foreknowledge of the plot."[9]

It is probable that Stanton and the Radicals dropped the case for a Confederate conspiracy, not because they had ceased to

George Templeton Strong, eds. Allan Nevins and Milton Halsey Thomas (New York: Macmillan, 1952) 4:15-16.
 5 *Official Records*, 49, pt. 2, 1116.
 6 Hans Trefousse, *The Radical Republicans* (New York: Knopf, 1969) 340-5.
 7 The statement was made in May 1866, *Southern Historical Society Papers*, 1/4 (April 1876): 325.
 8 Horace Greeley, *The American Conflict* (Hartford CT: O. D. Case, 1866) 2:748-9; Henry J. Raymond, *The Life and Public Service of Abraham Lincoln* (New York: Derby & Miller, 1865) 712-13.
 9 Thomas R. Turner, *Beware the People Weeping* (Baton Rouge: Louisiana State University Press, 1982) 68.

believe in it, but because they knew it would be impossible to prove. Even more important, it is likely they dropped the case because they knew that to continue to press it would indefinitely postpone reunion, possibly prevent it. Reunion could not possibly have taken place so quickly as it did had the public continued to believe Jefferson Davis and the others were Lincoln's murderers. The case a against them was given up for fear that pursuing it would lead to truths the nation would find it difficult or impossible to live with. Every generation until this one has concurred in the 1865 decision. The assassination was dismissed as the crime of a mad, revenge-seeking individual, and as such was not a subject for historical investigation.

In early May 1863 Union General George Stoneman led ten thousand mounted troops on a raid in the vicinity of Richmond at a time when Robert E. Lee's Confederate army was fifty miles away at Chancellorsville. From this raid, Lincoln learned and in his own hand informed General Joseph Hooker, commander of the Army of the Potomac, that the Rebel capital had been virtually undefended and that "our men, had they known it, could have safely gone in and burnt everything and brought us Jeff Davis." This document, a key to understanding the climactic event of 14 April 1865, is found in both Lincoln's *Collected Works* and the *Official Records of the War of the Rebellion*, but is conspicuously absent from Lincoln biographies and Civil War histories.[10]

The Union officer whose troops had been in the best position to enter Richmond during the Stoneman raid was H. Judson Kilpatrick, who never stopped dreaming about the opportunity he had had to win the war or talking about what he would do if he ever got another chance. He did get another chance. On 11 February 1864, when Lee's army was in winter quarters along the Rapidan River and Richmond's main defense force was temporarily in North Carolina, Lincoln ordered him to Washington.[11] After talking with Lincoln, Kilpatrick conferred with Stanton, and on 16 February he presented a plan of operations

---

[10] Roy P. Basler, ed. *The Collected Works of Abraham Lincoln* (New Brunswick, NJ: Rutgers University Press, 1952-1955) 6:202-3; *Official Records* 25:2:449.
[11] Basler, ed., *Collected Works*, 7: 178.

to General George Meade, now in command of the Army of the Potomac.

Kilpatrick's plan discussed and approved at the highest levels of the US government, was to take four thousand mounted troops to Richmond. While he entered the city from the north, a smaller detachment under Colonel Ulric Dahlgren, son of Lincoln's friend Admiral John A. Dahlgren, would enter it from the vulnerable south.[12] According to an officer on Meade's staff, the purpose of the raid was to liberate Union prisoners at Belle Isle and Libby prison "catch all the rebel M. C.'s [Members of Congress] that are lying loose, and make tracks to our nearest lines."[13]

Kilpatrick lost his nerve at the gates of Richmond. After minor skirmishing on 1 March, the sounds of which were heard in the office of an angry Jefferson Davis,[14] he fled down the peninsula to Fort Monroe. Dahlgren was ambushed and killed. On his body Rebels found papers announcing his intention of burning the city and capturing or killing Davis and his cabinet. Published throughout the Confederacy, the Dahlgren papers caused a sensation, most Southerners never doubting that Lincoln himself was responsible for the proposed atrocity. They had good reason for thinking so. Only the month before, the Richmond press had reported another attempted raid against Richmond that had had the same objectives.[15] In many other ways, Lincoln had demonstrated his contempt for the conventional rules of war by fighting under the black flag of "military necessity." As defined by US General Orders No. 100,

---

12 *Official Records*, 33:172-3.
13 Theodore Lyman, *Meade's Headquarters, 1863-1865* (Boston: Atlantic Monthly Press, 1922) 77-78.
14 J.B. Jones, *A Rebel Clerk's Diary* (New York: Old Hickory Bookshop, 1933) 2:164.
15 Joseph George, Jr., "'Black Flag Warfare': Lincoln and the Raids Against Richmond and Jefferson Davis," *Pennsylvania Magazine of History and Biography*, 115/3 (July 1991): 301. The Dahlgren papers and Lincoln's role in the Kilpatrick raid are discussed pp. 305-18. On the Dahlgren papers, see Davis F. Riggs, "The Dahlgren Papers Reconsidered," *Lincoln Herald*, 84/2 (Summer 1981); James O. Hall, "The Dahlgren Papers: A Yankee Plot to Kill President Davis," *Civil War Times Illustrated* (November 1983); and Emory Thomas, "The Kilpatrick-Dahlgren Raid," Ibid. (February, April 1978).

military necessity included all "those measures which are indispensable for securing the ends of the war...."[16]

Even before the Kilpatrick-Dahlgren raid, Davis had threatened retaliation for Lincoln's violations. After it, retaliation became a necessity. If Lincoln was fighting dirty, i. e., doing whatever was necessary to win, then Davis would have to fight dirty, too. As William C. Davis, the Confederate president's most scholarly biographer, puts it, Lincoln "had introduced a terrible new element into the war, a game at which more than one could play."[17]

Late in April 1864, the month after the Kilpatrick-Dahlgren raid, Davis sent Jacob Thompson of Mississippi and Clement C. Clay of Alabama to Canada with a million dollars in Secret Service gold. Their mission had two primary objectives. The first was to defeat Lincoln's bid for reelection in the fall by buying up some of the principal presses, especially in the old Northwest. The second was to encourage a Copperhead uprising by furnishing large sums of money for the purchase of weapons to societies like the Sons of Liberty, whose leaders traveled to Canada with their hands out and with largely fictional stories about the numbers and militancy of their members.[18]

Neither objective was achieved, although for the first, and let us hope the last time in our history, some newspapers in the area targeted by the Confederate government openly and flagrantly advocated the assassination of the tyrant Lincoln, thus creating an atmosphere as historian David E. Long observes, "ripe for explosion."[19]

---

[16] *Official Records*, ser. 3, vol. 3, 150.
[17] William C. Davis, *Jefferson Davis: The Man and His Hour* (New York: Harper Collins, 1991) 543.
[18] Oscar A. Kinchen, *Confederate Operations in Canada and the North* (North Quincy MA: Christopher Publishing Co., 1970), 38-9, chap. 3; William A. Tidwell, James O. Hall and David Winfred Gaddy, *Come Retribution: The Confederate Secret Service and the Assassination of Lincoln* (Jackson: University Press of Mississippi, 1988), chap. 8; William A. Tidwell, *April '65: Confederate Covert Action in the American Civil War* (Kent OH: Kent State University Press, 1995), chap. 5.
[19] *The Jewel of Liberty* (Mechanicsburg PA: Stackpole Books, 1994) 72. For examples of extremism in the press, see Frank Klement, "A Small Town Editor Criticizes Lincoln: A Study in Editorial Abuse,"

When Union victories in August and September virtually assured Lincoln's reelection, rebel strategists adopted a new policy to save their sinking cause. Under consideration for months, the new policy was to take the North out of the war by taking Lincoln out of the North. The president could be captured at his cottage at the Soldiers' Home north of Washington, escorted through the pro-Confederate countryside of southern Maryland to a boat on the Potomac, and held hostage in Richmond for a major and perhaps decisive concession. After the Stoneman raid of 1863, Lincoln had written of the ease with which Jefferson Davis could have been captured and Richmond burned. So capturing the president (either president) and burning his capital (either capital) were legitimate acts in the war of military necessity both sides were now fighting.

It has long been believed that John Wilkes Booth developed the plan to capture Lincoln on his own initiative, but recent scholarship has established beyond any reasonable doubt that Confederate leaders in Richmond and Canada formulated the plan and recruited Booth to carry it out.[20] Booth spent ten days in Montreal in October, staying at the same hotel as many rebel agents. He all but abandoned the stage during the 1864-1865 theatrical season, and devoted himself to assembling his action team, accumulating supplies, and establishing contacts in southern Maryland. By early 1865 his operation had become central to the military strategy of the Confederacy, and the code phrase for the main Confederate cipher system was changed from "Complete Victory" to "Come Retribution." Surely William A. Tidwell, James O. Hall, and David Winfred Gaddy, trailblazing scholars in the revision of assassination history, are justified in attaching significance to this change. It signaled that the man

---

Lincoln Herald, 54/2 (Summer 1952) and Klement, "Deuster as a Democratic Dissenter," *Transactions of the Wisconsin Academy of Sciences, Arts and Letters*, 55 (1966).

[20] One of the first historians to establish a link between the plan to capture and the Confederate government was John C. Brennan in "General Bradley T. Johnson's Plan to Abduct President Lincoln," *Chronicles of St. Mary's*, 22/11 (November 1974); 22/12 (December 1974); see also Brennan's "Confederate Spy—Captain Thomas Nelson Conrad," *Surratt Society News* (June and July 1977), and Tidwell etal, *Come Retribution*, 224-7, 262-4.

who was responsible for so many crimes against the South was about to get what was coming to him.[21]

Weeks passed and Booth found no realistic opportunity to capture Lincoln. By the end of March it was too late, for Union cavalry had blocked access to Richmond and there was no place to take a captive president. The Confederate States of America was about to be wiped off the map.

It is foreign to the way we have been taught to think of the Civil War, but why should not southern leaders now have concluded that the doctrine of military necessity, so often and so ruthlessly invoked against the South by Lincoln, justified direct attacks on him and members of his administration? Should Lincoln, a far greater tyrant than George III, be allowed to establish a centralized despotism on the ruins of the old federal union? The southern cause was just; it rested upon the principles of 1776, 1789, and 1798, which were sacred to the American experiment in limited government. If that experiment failed, the world's last best hope for freedom from oppressive government would perish from the earth.

Richmond fell on 3 April. The next day one of the occupying Union generals learned from a soldier in the Torpedo Bureau, a secret agency of the Rebel War Department, that two or three days before a party had been sent off on a secret mission the soldier believed was directed against the head of the United States government. It was ominous intelligence, for the Torpedo Bureau led the world in the invention and use of explosive devices: land mines, floating and submerged "torpedoes" for rivers and harbors, time bombs, and ingenious firewood and lump-of-coal mines. It was responsible for the mammoth explosion at Grant's headquarters in August 1864, and it had blown up arsenals supply depots, docks, and steamships. The general informed Lincoln, who was nearby aboard ship on the James River, but as he had in the past the president responded to the warning with a figurative shrug of his shoulders.[22]

---

[21] Ibid., 346-7.

[22] Ibid., 162-8; Milton F. Perry, *Infernal Machines: The Story of Confederate Submarine and Mine Warfare* (Baton Rouge: Louisiana State University Press, 1965), 131-8 and passim; Edward Hastings Ripley,

The soldier had known what he was talking about. Two days before the fall of Richmond, Thomas F. Harney, an experienced explosives expert, had been ordered to Mosby's Rangers to be infiltrated into Washington. In all probability, he was carrying more than fuses and detonators when he left, for William A. Tidwell has shown in his *April 1865: Confederate Covert Action in the Civil War* that on the same day President Davis approved Secretary of State Judah P. Benjamin's withdrawal of a large sum in gold from a special covert action account.[23] Why would an explosives expert liberally supplied with expense money be smuggled into Washington? Booth knew why. Early in April he had taken the train to New York and Boston and may have continued into Canada. Back in Washington on 8 or 9 April, he told a member of his action team, who later made a formal statement about it, that he had talked to men in New York who planned to blow up the White House when Lincoln and the cabinet or other top officials were present. They had the powder, but needed a specialist to set the mine and detonate it at the proper time.[24]

On 10 April, fifteen miles from Washington, Mosby's men skirmished with Union troops and Harney was taken prisoner, a loss to the Confederacy that one of the men called "irretrievable."[25] Booth may not have known what had happened to Harney, but he did know he was not present. That meant there would be no explosion at the White House to decapitate the US government. He apparently believed that the fate of the Con-

---

Vermont General, ed. by Otto Eisenschiml (New York: Devin-Adair, 1960), 306-8.

23 Tidwell, *April '65,* 162. All funds for clandestine operation had to be approved by Jefferson Davis; see also Tidwell etal, *Come Retribution,* 323-4.

24 Tidwell, et al, *Come Retribution,* 416-18; Tidwell, *April '65,* 163-4, 172. In a statement made on 1 May, George Atzerodt told James L. McPhail, Provost Marshal of Maryland, what he had learned from Booth about the Confederate plan. The statement was passed on to Atzerodt's attorney at the conspiracy trial, who made no use of it because without helping Atzerodt, it incriminated two other defendants. The statement was discovered in 1977 by Joan Chaconas, then president of the Surratt Society, among the papers of the attorney's grandson. With some errors of transcription, the text was published in the *Surratt Courier,* October 1988. A private collector now owns it.

25 Tidwell, *April '65,* 175; Tidwell et al, *Come Retribution,* 419-20.

federate States now rested in his hands alone, that only he could strike the blow that might yet save his country. Like other Rebels, including Jefferson Davis, he did not believe the Southern cause was lost. But it was obviously almost lost and, as he wrote in his memorandum book, "something decisive and great" must be done. He knew he could accomplish only a small part of what Harney was capable of, but was it not his duty to do whatever he could? So he ordered one of his men to kill Vice President Johnson, another to kill Secretary of State William H. Seward, and may have sent others after Stanton and Grant. He would take care of Lincoln himself. The others failed, he did not.

Mary Lincoln had thus been mistaken. They did not shoot the president, Booth did. But acting out of a desperate military necessity, they had armed his pistol.

8

THE CREATION OF AN AMERICAN MYTH: THE ASSASSINATION OF ABRAHAM LINCOLN

By Thomas R. Turner

The assassination of Abraham Lincoln by John Wilkes Booth vaulted the sixteenth president to the front ranks of American heroes and martyrs. The president's death, at the moment of Union triumph in the Civil War, has created a mythological figure of such enormous proportions that it is difficult, to this day, to separate the real man from the folk-myth legend which he has become.

Even the timing of Lincoln's murder, on Good Friday, was bound to evoke religious symbolism. Millions of Americans attended church services on Easter Sunday to hear clergymen attempt to explain and make sense of this calamity. One of the most common sermon themes preached was to equate the death of the president with that of Jesus. If Christ had died on Good Friday as the savior of the world, then Lincoln had suffered a similar fate as the savior of his country.[1]

Another strongly stated religious comparison was that of Lincoln to Moses. Similar to the leader of the Hebrews, Lincoln had reached the promised land, but God had not allowed him to cross over to it. In fact, many people argued that the reason for this was that Lincoln was too tender and merciful for the task of Reconstruction. Lincoln's work was completed and Andrew

---

[1] For an analysis of sermons preached, see Thomas R. Turner, *Beware the People Weeping: Public Opinion and the Assassination of Abraham Lincoln* (Baton Rouge: Louisiana State University Press, 1982) 77-89; David Chesebrough, *"No Sorrow Like Our Sorrow:" Northern Protestant Ministers and the Assassination of Lincoln* (Kent OH: Kent State University Press, 1994).

Johnson, who upon assuming office was making statements about harsh treatment for former rebels, was seen as the right person for the task ahead. If Lincoln played the role of Moses, Johnson was clearly a sterner Joshua to deal with the defeated South.[2]

It would be naive to assume that, if only Lincoln had lived, the problems of Reconstruction would have been negligible. However, the brief interval between the end of the war and the president's death, unleashed a period of joyous celebration. At Harvard College, J. L. Sibley captured this mood when he jotted in his diary, "The people are wild with enthusiasm at the news of the surrender of the rebel General Lee. It exceeds anything I have ever known. Another holiday in college. Illuminations, speeches, all round the country." In Washington, Secretary of War Stanton placed over his portico a clever arrangement of gas jets, which spelled out "PEACE." In Philadelphia, a citizen summed up his feelings to the editor of the *Philadelphia Evening Bulletin* in the following manner: "It sounds like hell let loose, but it feels like paradise regained."[3]

While this initial outburst would certainly have dissipated as it came up against the real world problems of reconstructing the Southern states, the fact that it occurred seemed to make the president's death that much more horrible for the Northern public. It was as if the nation had briefly let down its guard and, in that euphoric moment, the South had committed this last act of treachery. The violence which occurred was well foreshadowed in the poem "The Martyr" by Herman Melville, when he warned of the grief and anger which Lincoln's murder had engendered:

> He lieth in his blood
> The Father in his face;

[2] Charles J. Stewart, "A Rhetorical Study of the Reaction of the Protestant Clergy in the North to Lincoln's Assassination (Ph.D. dissertation, University of Illinois, 1963) 41.

[3] W. G. R., '09, (ed.), "Harvard and the Tragedy of 1865: Diary of John Langdon Sibley," in *Harvard Alumni Bulletin*, 26 April 1940, 899; Lloyd Lewis, *Myths After Lincoln* (New York: Harcourt Brace, 1929) 49; *Philadelphia Evening Bulletin*, 4 April 1865, 4.

They have killed him, the forgiver
The Avenger takes his place.
There is sobbing of the strong,
And a pall upon the land;
But the people in their weeping
Bare the iron hand:
Beware the People weeping
When they bare the iron hand.[4]

The reaction to the president's death was, of course, filled with both anger and sorrow. At Ford's Theatre there were cries to hang the assassin and burn the theater. A nearby shop-keeper, who tried to defend the theater personnel, had a rope placed around his neck and was barely rescued by the authorities from the angry mob. Theaters became such hated symbols that those in distant towns were placed under police protection for fear of destruction by fire. And, as the hearse bearing Lincoln's remains left from the Petersen House for the White House, one bystander was foolish enough to venture a shout for Jefferson Davis. He was set upon and nearly torn to pieces by the infuriated crowd.[5]

There was probably no more dramatic event, however, than that witnessed by Melville Stone, the General Manager of the Associated Press: "I made my way around the corner to the Matteson house...very soon I heard the crack of a revolver, and a man fell in the centre of the room. His assailant stood perfectly composed with a smoking revolver in his hand, and justified his action by saying: 'He said it served Lincoln right.' There was no arrest, no one would have dared arrest the man. He walked out a hero. I never knew who he was."[6]

The horror of the assassination affected both groups and individuals alike. One group which was particularly touched

---

4 Henning Cohen, ed., *The Battle Pieces of Herman Melville* (New York: Thomas Yoselof, 1964) 130.
5 W. J. Ferguson, *I Saw Booth Shoot Lincoln* (Boston: Houghton Mifflin, 1930) 58; Clara Morris, "Some Reflections of John Wilkes Booth," *McClure's Magazine*, 16 (1901): 303; Jim Bishop, *The Day Lincoln Was Shot* (New York: Harper and Bros., 1955) 213.
6 Unidentified newspaper clipping in Truman H. Bartlett Collection, Boston University.

was the black people for whom he had already become Father Abraham, the Great Emancipator. Navy Secretary Gideon Welles, who had sat in a chair at the foot of the dying president's bed in the Petersen House, said that the sorrow on the faces of blacks touched him most deeply, even though strong and brave men wept when he met them.[7]

Another group deeply affected was the assassin's family. Booth's sister, Asia Booth Clarke, recalled for the rest of her life the stigma which her brother's deed had caused, "The tongue of every man and woman was free to revile and insult us, every man's hand was raised against us; if we had friends they consoled with us in secret; none ventured near." A brother, Junius, who was appearing in Cincinnati, was saved from an angry mob by a hotel clerk who claimed he had left the city. Even so, a suspicious crowd watched the hotel for five days, and it was only then that he could be secretly spirited away. Even Edwin Booth, whose devotion to the Union was unquestioned, wrote to a friend Adam Badeau: "Oh! how little did I dream my boy, when on Friday night I was, as Sir Edward Mortimer, exclaiming 'Where is my honor now? Mountains of shame are piled upon me!' that I was not acting but uttering the fearful truth."[8]

Still other individuals, some at a very young age, chronicled the trauma which this event had caused. Jane Addams of Hull House fame wrote: "To my amazement I found my father in tears, something I had never seen before....The two flags, my father's tears and his impassioned statement that the greatest man in the world had died, constituted my initiation, my baptism, as it were, into the thrilling and solemn interests of a world lying quite outside the two white gate posts." Poet Katherine Lee Bates, who was five at the time, later wrote,

---

[7] Howard K. Beale, ed., *Diary of Gideon Welles* (New York: W. W. Norton, 1960) 2:290.

[8] Asia Booth Clarke, *The Unlocked Book: A Memoir of John Wilkes Booth by His Sister Asia Booth Clarke* (New York: G. P. Putnam's Sons, 1938) 131; "Edwin Booth and Lincoln With an Unpublished Letter by Edwin Booth," *Century Magazine*, 77 (1909): 920.

I heard it and hid me under the lilacs
The mystery to prod.
Lincoln! Lincoln! Abraham Lincoln!
And not one angel to catch the bullet!
What had become of God?

Even battle-hardened General Joshua L. Chamberlain, the hero of Little Round Top, noted during the Grand Review of the Army on 23 May, "But we miss the deep, sad eyes of Lincoln coming to review us after each sore trial. Something is lacking in our hearts now even in this supreme hour."[9]

One immediate conclusion reached by the public in 1865 was that the South was involved in Lincoln's death. While this judgment has seemed to puzzle later historians, nothing was more natural. Coming at the end of a conflict that had cost more than 620,000 lives, the president's death appeared to be one more horrible statistic to cap the tragedy. Thousands of people, including government officials, could not help but believe that Booth worked for the Confederacy. Secretary of the Navy Gideon Welles, a man not prone to profanity of any sort said simply, "Damn the rebels, this is their work."[10]

Very few Northerners, at least those who had supported the Union cause, had any trouble accepting President Johnson's May 2nd proclamation that "the atrocious murder of the late President Abraham Lincoln and the attempted assassination of Honorable W. H. Seward, Secretary of State, were incited, concerted, and procured by and between Jefferson Davis, Clement C. Clay, Beverly Tucker, George Sanders, W.C. Cleary, and other rebels and traitors." This view certainly hardened many people's attitudes toward Reconstruction. If the defeated

[9] Jane Addams, *Twenty Years at Hull House* (New York: 1912) 23; Katherine Lee Bates, *America The Dream* (New York: 1930) 107-9; Joshua L. Chamberlain, *The Passing of the Armies* (New York: 1915) 342, all quoted in Merrill D. Peterson, *Lincoln in American Memory* (New York: Oxford University Press, 1994) 5, 6, 23.

[10] Mrs. M. J. Welles' impression of the assassination, 14 April 1865, typescript in Gideon Welles Papers, Library of Congress.

rebels had murdered Lincoln, then they deserved no mercy at all.[11]

In fact, while Johnson would later have bitter clashes with the Radicals which would lead to his impeachment, in the aftermath of the murder, the vast majority of people were convinced that Johnson was the proper man to carry the country forward. Johnson was talking about hanging rebels and traitors and making treason odious, which caused Radical Ben Wade to say to him, "Johnson, we have faith in you. By the Gods, there will be no trouble now in running the government." These words would become bitterly ironical a couple of years later, but not in April 1865.[12]

Given the anger, violence, confusion, and frustration, there is little wonder that this chaotic situation had an equally large impact on the trials of the conspirators. While the United States has a strongly grounded tradition of civil trials in peacetime, military trials for civilians were not unusual during the Civil War. As Mark Neely has demonstrated so brilliantly in his Pulitzer prize winning study *The Fate of Liberty*, the Lincoln administration did not use military trials to stifle dissent, but generally to deal with people who had committed overt acts against the government in the midst of rebellion.[13]

With Lincoln dead, a military trial seemed to many people a logical way to try conspirators, who were seen as tools of the Confederate government. It was also perceived by the public as the means to get to the bottom of a vast conspiracy. While there was no Warren Commission to investigate the assassination events, it was felt that the military court, with its wider rules of evidence, would leave no stone unturned and no question unanswered.

An examination of the trial testimony reveals that much of the evidence was geared toward proving Confederate involve-

---

[11] *New York Herald*, 4 May 1865, 1. For newspapers which accepted the truth of the government proclamation see *New York Times*, 4 May 1865, 1, 4; *Gettysburg Adams Sentinel*, 9 May 1865, 2.

[12] George W. Julian, *Political Recollections, 1840-1872*, (Chicago: Jensen, McClung, 1884) 255, 257.

[13] Mark E. Neely, Jr., *The Fate of Liberty*, (New York: Oxford University Press, 1991).

ment in Lincoln's murder, rather than to demonstrate individual guilt or innocence. Many witnesses testified to alleged statements made by Jefferson Davis, as well as plots to spread Yellow Fever, poison reservoirs, and burn Northern cities. Ministers also reinforced this view in the hundreds of sermons preached, rarely mentioning Booth by name, but castigating Southerners and slavery for having precipitated the assassin's actions.[14]

In a certain sense, the verdict of the Military Commission was a symbolic punishment for the South, as well as these alleged Southern conspirators. Nonetheless, the argument that the military tribunal was particularly vindictive and bloodthirsty does not stand up to careful scrutiny. Five of the conspirators had definitely been involved with Booth in either a kidnapping plot or the murder; and, in Ed Spangler's case, people suspected that the assassin had help in the theater. There was also ample evidence, albeit some of it circumstantial, that Mary Surratt, who was a strong Southern sympathizer, was at the least an accessory before the fact. Dr. Mudd, whose protests that he did not recognize Booth rang hollow in light of Booth's prior visit to his home, was also, in the same sense, technically an accessory after the fact. If the Military Commission's recommendations had been followed, the only conspirators executed would have been David Herold, who was found with Booth in Garrett's Barn; George Atzerodt, who admitted that Booth had asked him to kill Vice-President Johnson; and Lewis Payne, who had assaulted Secretary Seward, leaving his household in shambles. In the heated circumstances of 1865, it is highly unlikely that a civil jury would have been any more discriminating than these military officers were.[15]

Of course, this perception of the bloodthirstiness of the military court was reinforced by the hung jury and failure to retry John Surratt in 1867. It was extremely easy to argue that, since John Surratt was not convicted based on the same evidence

---

[14] See Turner, *Beware the People Weeping: Public Opinion and the Assassination of Abraham Lincoln*, 77-79, 125-37.

[15] For the trial testimony see Benn Pitman, *The Assassination of President Lincoln and the Trial of the Conspirators* (New York: Funk and Wagnall's, 1954) 17-18.

which was introduced in 1865, that the major significant difference was trial by a military court versus a civil one.

In reality, trials are often greatly influenced by the times in which they occur.[16] By 1867, the immediate chaotic aftermath of 1865 had largely subsided. Viewed in this calmer light, the evidence against John Surratt seemed a lot less convincing. The defense was able to introduce witnesses who contradicted testimony placing Surratt in front of Ford's Theatre on 14 April. When additional testimony put Surratt in upstate New York on 13 April (and probably 14 April), the prosecution had to resort to rather convoluted railroad schedules to show that he would have been able to return to Washington by the time of Lincoln's murder. This evidence caused reasonable doubt on the part of some jurors and the case began to unravel. It was no wonder that the jury could not agree on a verdict, not because they were civilians, but because in calmer times they could scrutinize the evidence more carefully. In 1865, a military or civil jury, would probably have seen this same evidence as compelling proof of John Surratt's guilt.[17]

This trial, however, did become one of the more famous ones in American history. In 1866 the Supreme Court decided in Ex parte Milligan that civilians should not be tried in military courts while civil courts are open and functioning. This has led to blanket charges that the military trial was retroactively nullified. (Notwithstanding this, some alleged German spies were tried and executed by military court in Washington during World War II.)

Interestingly, by 1867, there was some speculation that Andrew Johnson might have been involved in his predecessor's death. (A play entitled *McBird* was written after John Kennedy's death attributing similar involvement to Lyndon Johnson.) The enigmatic card which Booth left at the National Hotel (Don't

---

[16] This should not be news to us, for in modern America it is apparently increasingly difficult to hold the rich and famous responsible for anything, as witnessed by the trial of O.J. Simpson or the Menendez brothers, although the latter were convicted in a subsequent trial and Simpson was held liable in a civil proceeding.

[17] *Trial of John H. Surratt in the Criminal Court For the District of Columbia, Hon. George P. Fisher Presiding*, 2 vols. (Washington, DC: United States Government Printing Office, 1867).

wish to disturb you, are you at home?), which may not even have been meant for Johnson, led to speculation that, since Johnson had benefited the most from Lincoln's death, that he was behind it. General Benjamin Butler, during the course of the John Surratt trial, had managed to have a select committee appointed, with himself as chairman, to investigate the assassination. While the committee did take some testimony and received letters from those who said they could implicate the president, nothing came of it. There were also rumors, which turned out to be untrue, that Surratt was being offered a deal if he would link Booth with Johnson.[18]

Johnson's historical reputation has not been very good because of his clashes with the Radical Republicans and his impeachment, even though he managed to avoid being removed from office. While his stature has been diminished, a fair number of contemporaries were apparently doubly disgusted with Johnson, believing these rumors of his involvement in Lincoln's murder.[19]

The assassination did have a way of damaging reputations and Johnson's was not the only one to suffer. Paradoxically, his nemesis, Secretary of War Edwin Stanton, also had his name tarnished as well. In reality, Lincoln and Stanton were close both politically and personally. Not only did they share adjoining summer cottages on the grounds of the Soldier's Home, where they played with each other's children, but they also shared a close working relationship.

Stanton was the harsher of the two men but he could sometimes see the virtue in a kind act, although he could not personally carry it out because it would undermine military

---

[18] Barbara Garson, *McBird* (New York: Grove Press, 1966); Hans L. Trefousse, "Belated Revelations of the Assassination Committee," *Lincoln Herald*, 58 (1956): 13-16.

[19] See for example *Springfield* (MA) *Daily Republican*, 28 January 1867, 2; Howard K. Beale, ed., *The Diary of Edward Bates, 1859-1866*, Vol. IV of the Annual Report of the American Historical Association, 1930 (Washington, DC: United States Government Printing Office, 1933) 493.

Andrew Johnson
(Courtesy of *The Abraham Lincoln Museum*)

discipline. He would, therefore, send the petitioners to Lincoln. On the other hand, when Lincoln saw that he could not undertake some action, he would dispatch the petitioners to Stanton, who would turn them down. In both cases, the president maintained his kindly image, and Stanton's reputation as being vindictive increased. Stanton played this role gladly to shield Lincoln, even if his own historical reputation might suffer.[20]

And suffer it did, because as Reconstruction ended without the complete accomplishment of the Radical's goals, the ideals that the Radicals had espoused went out of fashion. Historians portrayed the Radicals as partisan, petty, mean, and vindictive men who had wreaked havoc on a prostrate South. In Stanton's case, he was charged with having used Lincoln's assassination as an excuse to unleash a reign of terror to facilitate the Radical's program. This criticism culminated in the twentieth century when it was argued that Stanton hated Lincoln so much that he had engineered the president's death.[21]

Unfortunately, to this day and despite the best efforts of historians, Stanton's reputation still remains clouded. There is an irony that two men, Johnson and Stanton, who were polls apart ideologically and politically, both had their reputations tarnished by Lincoln's murder.

If Lincoln's death affected those who lived through it in a variety of ways, the effect has lingered throughout the next 131 years of American history. A journalist captured this very perceptively when he wrote of the murder: "It has made it impossible to speak the truth of Abraham Lincoln hereafter." Horace White observed, "The most striking fact of our time, of a psychological kind, is the growth of Lincoln's fame since the earth closed over his remains." Perhaps it was inevitable that the Savior of the Union and the Great Emancipator would have become a folkhero in any case, but the trend was accelerated by

[20] Benjamin Thomas and Harold Hyman, *Stanton, The Life and Times of Lincoln's Secretary of War* (New York: Alfred A. Knopf, 1962) 381-401.
[21] William A. Dunning, *Essays on the Civil War and Reconstruction and Related Topics* (Freeport NY: Books For Libraries Press, 1971, reprint of 1897 edition); Claude Bowers, *The Tragic Era, The Revolution After Lincoln* (New York: Blue Ribbon Books, 1929).

his martyrdom. The man whose election had precipitated secession and civil war entered the American Pantheon.[22]

It has been maintained that Americans were searching for just such a folk-hero as Abraham Lincoln. As people of a revolutionary tradition, we not only separated ourselves from our English heritage politically, but also culturally. Like other revolutionary peoples we had to reinvent our past. Part of this was accomplished by glorifying the colonial and revolutionary periods. The *Mayflower*, Plymouth Rock, John Smith and Pocahontas, all became instant icons. So, too, did George Washington, who became both man and monument as the father of his country. Washington, however, was not an entirely satisfactory folk-hero. The first president was an Olympian folk-god, one who could be admired and worshipped from afar but who was not really approachable.

Abraham Lincoln thus became a folk-hero for the common man. Born in a log cabin, in humble circumstances, he rose to the highest office in the land, saved the Union, freed the slaves, and was struck down at the height of his glory. This is the stuff of which legends are made.[23]

While we lack the space to deal with all of the ramifications of this mythology, there are numerous illustrations of it. One of the most persistent myths is that the assassin survived Garrett's Barn and that someone else died in his place. The most recent manifestation of this was the attempt to exhume Booth's remains from the Green Mount cemetery in Baltimore. Even though this request was supported by descendants of Edwin Booth, the court ruled that there were no grounds to believe that the body was not that of the assassin.[24]

Lloyd Lewis in a very perceptive but underrated study, argued that the belief that John Wilkes Booth survived Garrett's Barn is not rooted in reality but also in folk-myth. In traditional mythology, the slayer of the folk-god could not die an easy

[22] Quoted in Peterson, *Lincoln in American Memory*, 21, 41.
[23] Henry Steele Commager, "The Search For a Usable Past," *American Heritage* 16 (February 1965): 4-9, 90-96.
[24] *New York Times*, 12 May 1995, 14; 18 May 1995, 1; 20 May 1995, 1; 21 May 1995, 34; *Boston Globe*, 17 May 1995, 14; 18 May 1995, 7.

death but had to wander the world alone and friendless to do penance for his sins.[25]

In fact, there seems to be some sort of universal theme at work here. There have been many books and articles written about Lee Harvey Oswald doubles, and one author was so persistent in his claim that the "real" Oswald was not killed in Dallas that the body was exhumed after a messy legal battle between Oswald's brother and his widow, Marina. Jesse James's grave was also recently opened to an equal amount of fanfare. In both cases, the remains were positively identified, but this will probably not silence the true believers any more than people will cease to believe that Booth survived Garrett's Barn.[26]

Lincoln also became an historical figure who was treated like very few others. One of the recent debates that has raged about Lincoln is whether he had the disease Marfan Syndrome, and if bits of bone fragment should be used to generate DNA to test for this disease. Marfans is a connective tissue disease, marked by droopy eyes, sunken chest, deformities of fingers and toes, and which is almost always fatal. Since it is also hereditary and passed on through males in a family, it has also been suggested that this is the reason three of Lincoln's four sons died at an early age.

Even without DNA testing, historians, as well as medical doctors, have demonstrated to a fair degree of probability that Lincoln did not have the disease. The president was in far too robust condition and, with the exception of his eyes, lacked all of the other symptoms. But that is not the point. With Lincoln, we are insatiable to learn everything we can, even down to his genetic structure. It would be difficult to imagine such morbid curiosity about any other American president. And, even if Lincoln did suffer from the disease, it had no known impact on

[25] Lewis, *Myths After Lincoln*, 347-356.
[26] Michael Eddowes, *The Oswald File* (New York: Clarkson N. Potter, 1977); *New York Times*, 5 October 1981, 1, 16; *New York Times*, 20 July 1995, 1, 25 September 1995, 16; *Atlanta Journal and Constitution*, 16 September 1995, 1; *Boston Globe*, July 18, 1995, 8.

his presidency, in the manner that strokes and heart disease did on the presidencies of Wilson or Eisenhower.[27]

Lincoln also became an enigmatic figure, with many groups claiming him as one of their own. Was Lincoln a true Christian, who accepted Jesus after Gettysburg and the death of his son Willie, or was he an atheist and skeptic as claimed by his law partner William Herndon? It is impossible to deny him his place as the Great Emancipator and yet, in the late nineteenth and early twentieth century, white racist groups combing his utterances adopted him as a kindred spirit. Similarly, prohibitionists have touted Lincoln as a teetotaler, while pro-liquor forces have portrayed him as drinking wine, albeit in moderate amounts.[28]

There are very few historical figures who can be seen as all things to all people in the manner in which Lincoln has been portrayed. One of the reasons for this ambivalence was Lincoln's reticence about his personal life and his inclination to secrecy. The consensus of many who knew him was that he was the most secretive man they had ever known. Historian Richard Hofstadter has argued that one of the creators of this Lincoln legend was Lincoln himself. Lincoln saw the virtue of the rags-to-riches myth in American politics and used it very effectively in his campaigns.[29]

Even the historiography of the assassination has mirrored some of the major trends in American history. Indeed, a cottage industry of Lincoln assassination books has grown up, the same way it has around the death of John Kennedy. As noted, at the end of the war, nothing was more natural than to assume that

---

[27] Gabor S. Boritt and Adam Boritt, "Lincoln and the Marfan Syndrome: The Medical Diagnosis of a Historical Figure," *Civil War History*, 29 (September 1983): 212-229. For a recent discussion of the ethics of genetic research, as well as an assessment as to whether it is possible to utilize Lincoln's genetic materials to test for Marfan Syndrome see Glen W. Davidson, "Abraham Lincoln and the DNA Controversy," *Journal of the Abraham Lincoln Association*, 17 (Winter 1996):1-26.

[28] Stephen B. Oates, *Abraham Lincoln, The Man Behind the Myths* (New York: Harper and Row, 1984).

[29] Oates, *Abraham Lincoln, The Man Behind the Myths*, 35-36; Richard Hofstadter, *The American Political Tradition and the Men Who Made It* (New York: Vintage Books, 1948).

the South had been involved. People would have been incredulous if the authorities had announced that the South had no role in the president's death. After all, the Warren Commission did not put to rest the public's belief of conspiracy in the death of JFK.

It was also only a rather short step from the belief that the Radical Republicans had used the murder to further their vindictive policies to attributing to them more sinister motives. In the 1930s and 1940s, beginning with Otto Eisenschiml, authors began to hint that the Radicals hate was so strong that they had engineered the president's death. While Americans often tend to date their mistrust of government to the assassination of John Kennedy, the Vietnam War, or Watergate, this belief that the president was betrayed by members of his administration predates our modern anxieties by several generations.[30]

While Eisenschiml merely raised questions, sometimes refusing to take credit for the implied answers, others rushed in to fill in the blanks. There have been allegations of elaborate plots involving Stanton or head of the National Detective police, Lafayette Baker. One book even charged that Secretary Seward, who was attacked, was himself involved and that a co-plotter took advantage to try and eliminate him as well.[31]

The 1977 book and movie the *Lincoln Conspiracy* argued that Booth was a tool of the Radicals and northern businessmen and, of course, Booth survives Garrett's Barn. The impact of a sensational movie, along the lines of Oliver Stone and *JFK*, should not be underestimated. One of my colleagues recently told me she has never seen the movie *JFK* and does not plan to. Having read very little of the literature about Kennedy's murder, she feared that Stone's version would insidiously become her own.[32]

---

[30] Otto Eisenschiml, *Why Was Lincoln Murdered?* (Boston: Little, Brown, 1937).
[31] Vaughan Shelton, *Mask For Treason* (Harrisburg: The Stackpole Co., 1965).
[32] David Balsiger and Charles E. Sellier, Jr., *The Lincoln Conspiracy* (Los Angeles: Schick Sunn Classic Books, 1977).

Her concerns are well founded based on a statement by Danny Arce, one of the witnesses to the Kennedy murder in Dealey Plaza:

> I have read and heard so many things it mixes together. You don't know if it's your own memory or it's somebody else's. We all read a lot of things, and sometimes inadvertently adopt things we hear from others. It's hard to separate the two, and can get real confusing trying to figure out what you remember without having your memory colored by everything that has come out.[33]

Recently, we have come full circle with William Tidwell, David Gaddy, and James Hall, arguing that Jefferson Davis and the Confederates actually were behind Booth's plot to kidnap Lincoln, which eventually culminated in his murder. If Tidwell and his associates are correct, then the public in 1865 had the answer to the crime all along.

The authors believe that early in the war, the Confederacy, at both the national and state levels, developed an extensive intelligence service in an attempt to overcome the Northern advantages in manpower and industrial base. Relying on agents within Washington and numerous operatives in Maryland and Virginia, messages, mail, and personnel could be rapidly transferred between North and South. The Confederates also turned to less conventional warfare, planting agents in Canada to plan raids on northern soil, dabbling in the use of torpedoes and land mines, or trying to spread diseases such as Yellow Fever. Among the Confederates most important intelligence gatherers was General John Singleton Mosby who, despite his dashing and romantic reputation as the "Gray Ghost," commanded a regularly organized unit which, like most cavalry units, conveyed accurate intelligence information to the Confederate government and field commanders alike.

---

[33] Gerald Posner, *Case Closed: Lee Harvey Oswald and the Assassination of JFK* (New York: Random House, 1993) 235.

After the Kilpatrick-Dahlgren raid on Richmond, when papers found on the body of Ulrich Dahlgren allegedly revealed a plot to kill Davis and members of his government, the Confederates, in retaliation, developed a plan to capture Lincoln. The already established intelligence network was extended and action teams, including those of John Wilkes Booth who was a Confederate agent, were assembled to carry out the plan. Ultimately in April, 1865, with the South on the verge of defeat, the Confederacy resorted to murder when Thomas Harney, a member of Mosby's command, was dispatched to blow up the White House. Harney was captured but Booth, who was aware of his plan, decided to duplicate it as best he could by killing the president and members of his cabinet.

It was no accident that Booth and Herold were aided in their flight by Confederate soldiers Mortimer Ruggles, Absalom Bainbridge, and Willie Jett, who were part of the forces which were on the lookout to help the conspirators even after the plot had turned to murder. When Booth died at Garrett's barn, however, the intelligence forces supposedly melted away and were disbanded, and naturally everyone kept quiet. Confederate envoy George Sanders, who had met Booth in Canada and perhaps even encouraged him to murder Lincoln, began a campaign to provide perjured testimony at the trial of Booth's alleged co-conspirators. When this testimony was discovered to be perjured, it drew attention away from Confederate involvement in the murder.[34]

Tidwell's thesis, which is based largely on circumstantial evidence, has met with skepticism from many historians. Critics argue that his portrait of intelligence operations seems more firmly grounded in the twentieth century than the nineteenth. As Mark Neely has noted, while no age has been completely free from barbarism, nations in the nineteenth century may have been as little likely to commit assassinations as in any age before or since. While capturing a chief executive might be considered legitimate in time of war, Victorian gentlemen such

---

[34] William A. Tidwell, James O. Hall and David Winfred Gaddy, *Come Retribution, The Confederate Secret Service and the Assassination of Lincoln* (Jackson: University of Mississippi Press, 1988); Tidwell, *April '65* (Kent OH: Kent State University Press, 1995).

as Jefferson Davis, are extremely unlikely perpetrators of political murder. The enemy order of battle, that is how many troops the other side had and their disposition, could easily be gained by a man with binoculars on the top of a high hill. Other information could be gleaned by interrogating prisoners or even reading the newspapers. The type of strategic intelligence which military analysts specialize in now was undreamed of by nineteenth century intelligence operatives. Even the CIA today employs far more Ph.D.s with degrees in economics, history, political science or languages than exotic field operatives, but the average person's view of intelligence has been colored by the many books and movies of the James Bond variety.[35]

It has also been questioned whether Booth, who in this scenario was a Confederate super agent, would really have been chosen to be such a key player in Confederate intelligence. While his profession allowed him freedom of movement, Booth seemed to have a rather loose tongue and the actor's flair for the dramatic. When he killed Lincoln, even if he was only acting in conjunction with what he thought the Confederate authorities wanted, he ran a grave risk of capture and exposure of the plot.

In cases such as this, the historian should demand more than circumstantial evidence. As noted, the reputation of Secretary of War Stanton was permanently tarnished by conspiracy charges against him. Similarly, there should be a major re-evaluation of Jefferson Davis if he resorted to political murder, no matter what the provocation. If such a re-examination is to occur, it should be based on a very high standard of proof. The burden to sustain sensational charges is clearly on those who make them and not the other way around.

It appears that Tidwell, whose work is largely based on circumstantial evidence and intelligence insights he claims to possess from his work with the CIA, is influenced as much by the tenor of the times as the facts. We live in an age which has

[35] Mark E. Neely, Jr., Review of *Come Retribution, The Confederate Secret Service and the Assassination of Lincoln* by William A. Tidwell, with James O. Hall and David Winfred Gaddy in *American Historical Review* (June 1990): 913-914.

become so suspicious about the powers of governments and their intelligence agencies that many people cannot believe that an assassination could be the work of a few individuals, no matter what the evidence might be.

To die randomly at the hands of an individual or small group, in much the same way that people die all the time in the United States in drive-by shootings, is much too irrational a view of life for many Americans. In a perverse sort of way, a conspiracy restores some order to a world of chaos.

However, as regards the Lincoln assassination, perhaps we should not be surprised that we have come full circle. There are some figures in American history who have one or two standard biographies written about them and we are satisfied. This has never been the case with Abraham Lincoln. The secrecy of the man certainly contributed to this, as well as the martyrdom he suffered. His assassination struck some deep psychological nerve in the American psyche which has caused him to be reinterpreted from generation to generation, for as Merrill Peterson writes in his conclusion to *Lincoln in American Memory*,

As everything about the war lived in memory, so did Lincoln. And his assassination in the hour of victory stabbed at the nation's heart. He was a man of mystery and paradox: raw and folksy, yet sturdy and dignified; a laughing friend, a melancholy stranger, 'hard as rock and soft as drifting fog,' as Sandburg said. There was so much of him, he seemed fated to remain forever unknown.[36]

---

[36] Peterson, *Lincoln in American Memory*, 395.

Book design by Marc A. Jolley.
Jacket Design by Jim Burt.
Photographs courtesy of The Abraham Lincoln Museum at
      Lincoln Memorial University in Harrogate, Tennessee.
Text font: Book Antiqua.
Printed and bound by Edwards Brothers.